Quilty Needlepoint Needlepoint Projects Inspired by Quilts
The Small Projects

Janet M Perry

© 2023 Napa Needlepoint
630 Tisdale Ave.
Mare Island, CA 94592

ISBN: 9798362057923

Library of Congress Catalog Number: 20333922065

All rights reserved. No portion of this book may be reproduced in any way without permission of the author.

Pictures throughout the book are of needlepoint canvases stitched & photographed by the author. The charts, diagrams, photos, and projects are copyright Napa Needlepoint.

Table of Contents

Introduction	5
Poinsettia Ornament	6
Rainbow Blocks	8
Firestorm	11
Cloisonné Five Patch	15
Amish Double Four Patch	17
Holiday Rickrack Mini-sock	19
Autumn Leaf Diamond	23
Sunburst	26
Amish Bargello Mini-sock	28
Scrappy Squares	31
Tulips	33
Rhodes Heart	35
Wedding Day	37
Scrap Basket	39
Bookshelf	41
Jonquil	44
Preppy Heart	49
Wild Thing	53
Offset Flower	58
Triangle Christmas Tree	62
Heart Star	65
Pyramids Mini-sock	68
Houses	71

Swirling Stars 74

Christmas Squares 77

Amish Star 80

Introduction

I've adored quilts since I was a girl and married into a family that had generations of quilters. Although my grandmother made lovely quilts and we have beautiful quilts made by my husband's grandmother and great-grandmother, I am no great shakes when it comes to quilting. I've made three quilts, all crib quilts, all machine pieced and quilted.

Instead I've taken my love of quilts and quilt blocks into making needlepoint versions of quilts. I've adopted quilt blocks and whole quilts of many kinds into needlepoint projects. This book is the first volume of a series of books on quilty needlepoint.

The projects in this book are all small. They can be ornaments, small projects, or inserts for self-finishing items. Most of the projects are designed to use odds & ends of thread. You'll learn about how to do this in the next section of the introduction.

It's time to go to your stash and stitch!

Scrap Bag Projects

Many of the projects are designed to use the odds and ends of thread you have. I call this Scrap Bag Needlepoint after the quilts that use bits and pieces of fabric. These kinds of quilts strive to achieve a random look called "scrappy."

As needlepointers, it can be hard to create a scrappy look. This process is made much easier if you follow these guidelines. We often end up with tail ends of threads from kits, the last yard or so from a skein, and samples you might get from shops. These can beautifully form your scrap bag.

First, edit your choices by only picking colors that fit your color scheme. For example Preppy Heart uses pink and lime. Other shades of red and green or other colors won't work in this project as I stitched it. Other designs, such as Wedding Day, don't require specific colors. Here you can use any colors you like. If you want to use a specific color scheme, edit your colors first.

To fill in the scrap blocks, pick a thread at random. Use this thread and stitch one section of the block. It could be a square, rectangle, or a portion of the block. Once this is complete, park your thread in the margin until you are ready to use it again.

The tricky part comes as you stitch more blocks. When you pick a second or subsequent thread, it should be in contrast to any colors that meet it. The same color should not appear in the same row in any direction. If you must use the same thread again in the same row, the two blocks should be far from each other.

You can, and should, use the parked thread to stitch another scrap block. I'll warn you though; this does not make for neat backs.

Some of the quilts, such as Tulips, have blocks that use two scrap bag threads. When you have this circumstance do not use the same color combination in the same places in more than one block.

Poinsettia Ornament

There is a tradition, probably not that old, of making special quilts for Christmas. This is the first of the projects in this book that are based on these quilts. A square design, probably a wall hanging, it features a bold poinsettia with two different colors of red thread. Small leaves poke out from behind the flower. A gold center completes the flower. There are two borders around the design to complete the ornament.

Materials

1 spool or card gold metallic ribbon (model uses Kreinik 1/16" ribbon in 002)
1 skein each thread of your choice in white, green, dark red, red (model uses Silk & Ivory)
7 inch square 18-mesh mono needlepoint canvas

Step-by-step Instructions

Stitch the main part of the ornament in Straight Stitches according to the chart on the next page. Follow the picture of the model for color placement. The stitches will vary in length from over 1 thread to over five threads.

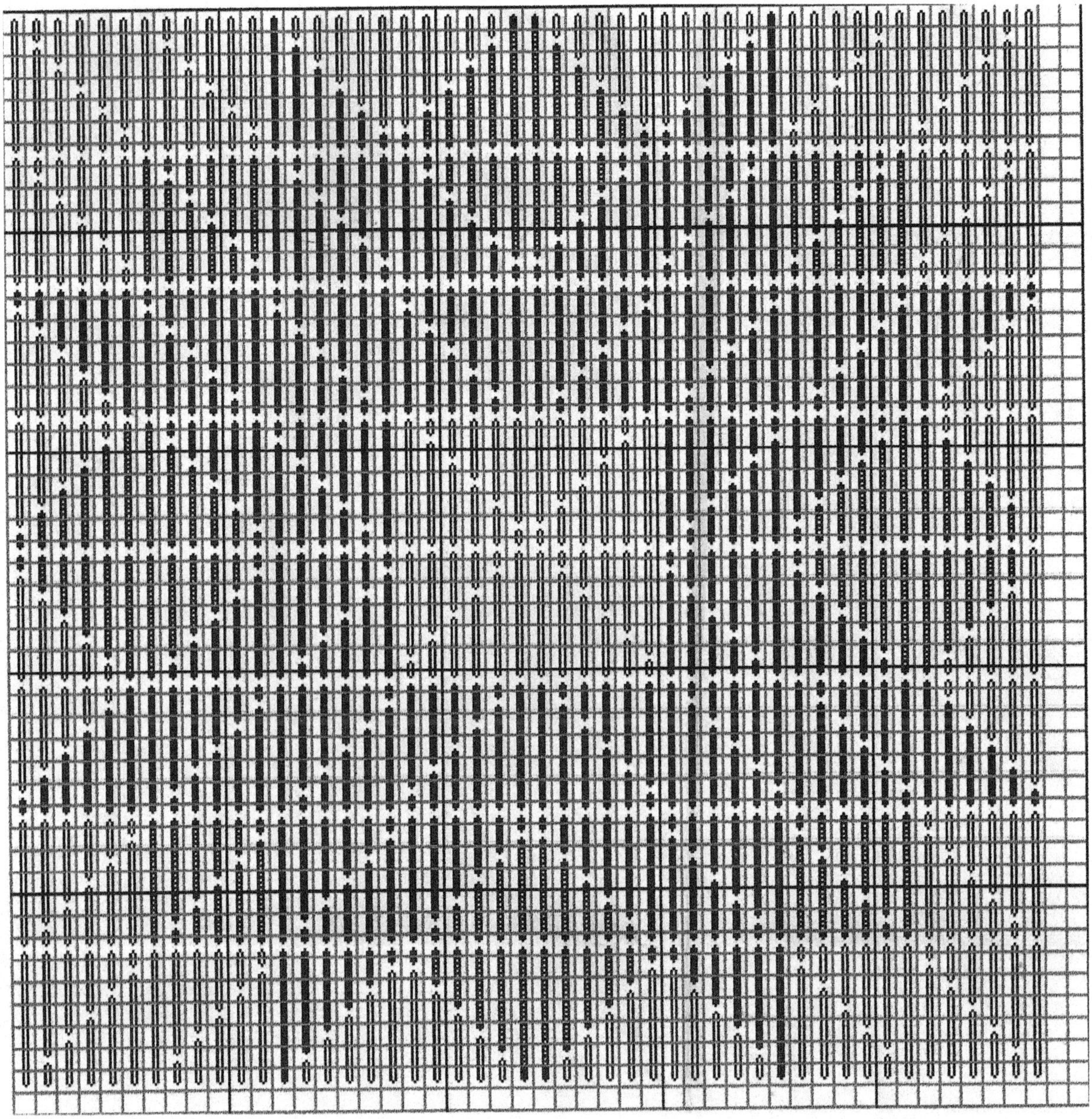

Once the center is stitched, stitch the gold border in **Straight Gobelin,** below left, using the gold ribbon. The corners should be mitered, below right.

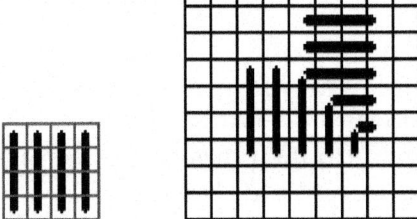

Finish the ornament with a single row of **Continental** around the ornament

Rainbow Blocks

This project is based on a quilt layout I found on Pinterest, from Felt Magnet. I loved the Lego-like feel of the groups of four bricks, but I wasn't crazy about the colors. Instead I used two sets of complementary colors with the pairs across from each other. I picked different threads in those colors for each group of four bricks.

Materials

>10 1-yard lengths of thread each in two colors, mostly solid colors
>15 1-yard lengths of thread each in two colors, mostly solid colors
>7 inch square 18-mesh mono needlepoint canvas

Adapting the Quilt to Needlepoint

As you can see from the project map on page 10, this design is made up of rectangles that are two units in one direction and one in the other. Some possibilities would be Brick (1×2) or Elongated Smyrna Crosses (2×4). The stitch you pick will, of course, have implications for the finished size of the project.

The project is an eighteen brick square. That makes it very easy to convert to needlepoint on 18-mesh canvas.

* If your stitch is 1 thread in the short direction (Brick), the finished size will be 1 inch.
* If your stitch is 2 threads in the short direction (Elongated Smyrna), the finished size will be 2 inches.
* .If your stitch is 3 threads in the short direction (Cashmere), the finished size will be 3 inches.

Because I wanted the piece to be ornament-sized but still have a strong impact of color, I chose to use the **Cashmere Stitch**, below, which is 3×6 threads.

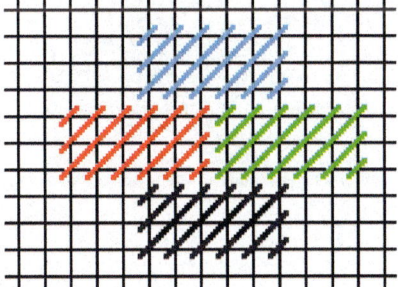

Step-by-step Instructions

I used the quilt layout, page 10, as my pattern and this Cashmere Stitch, above, as the stitch. I started with the green quadrant, placing the first unit horizontally. That makes green a "small" quadrant with six complete brick units (four Cashmeres) and four partial units (three Cashmeres).

The two "large" quadrants are stitched next, completing one before starting the other. These quadrants have ten complete units and five individual Cashmeres. In these areas because I was using two colors, I alternated the colors row by row.

Finally, I stitched the red quadrant that is another "small" quadrant.

It's exactly 3" so it can be put into a 3" square frame or finished as an ornament.

10

Firestorm

Flames and smoke-filled skies have inspired this needlepoint. While I didn't have the shiny threads to do this quilt in the dramatic colors of fires at night, this unusual combination of pale gray and orange creates an image that could also be of autumn. If you want it to be more like a sunny autumn day, change the gray to light blue and add more yellows and reds to the oranges.

Materials

7×8 inch square 18-mesh canvas
1 skein light grey thread (model uses Vineyard Silk)
up to 24 orange threads from scrap pile (yellow-orange, orangish-browns, and golds can also be used)

Step-by-step Instructions

The project has 24 blocks, arranged in four columns of six blocks each. Each patch has four rows that are unevenly divided between grey and orange, making a block divided along the diagonal. The blocks are arranged so that they create feathered zigzag rows. The diagram below shows one block. The patches are all three threads wide and are stitched in **Reverse Diagonal Gobelin** or **Diagonal Gobelin**.

Each of the rows in the patches ends in a triangle. These triangles, no matter what color is used, always have three stitches. That makes the small patch where the two triangles meet a rectangle instead of a Scotch Stitch square. This is essential for the balanced look of the quilt portrait.

There are four blocks:

* Block A, below, has orange on the left and grey on the right with orange increasing in size as you go up. It is in Reverse Diagonal Gobelin.

* Block B, next page top, has orange on the left and grey on the right with orange decreasing in size as you go up. It is in Diagonal Gobelin.

* Block C, next page middle, has orange on the right and grey on the left with orange decreasing in size as you go up. It is in Reverse Diagonal Gobelin.

* Block D, next page bottom, has orange on the right and grey on the left with orange increasing in size as you go up. It is in Diagonal Gobelin.

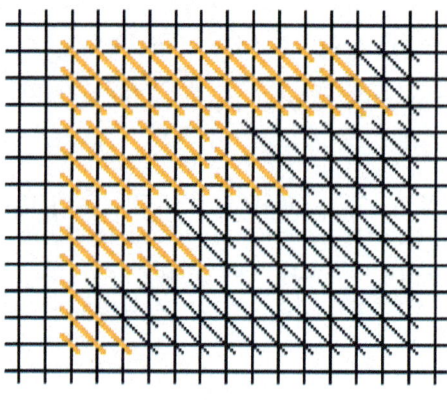

Block A

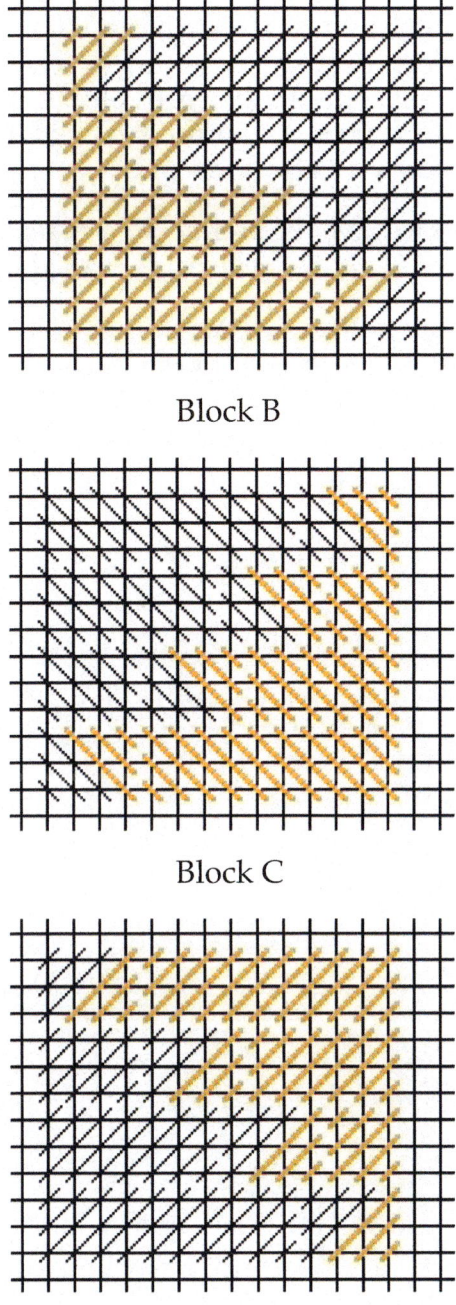

Block B

Block C

Block D

The project is easiest if you stitch all the blocks in one color in one column at once, stitching zigzag row by zigzag row. Begin at either lower corner, with the orange patches, Stitch all the orange patches in that column, then the column of grey patches to complete these blocks. Reverse the order for the next column of blocks. The third column repeats the first column and the fourth column repeats the second.

When picking your colors try to have different colors or textures in adjoining blocks. If you have threads that are different in color or texture, spread them around the design.

Columns 1 and 3 are, from bottom to top: A,B,A,B,A,B.
Columns 2 and 4 are, from bottom to top: C,D,C,D,C,D.

Cloisonné Five Patch

This Plastic Canvas Christmas ornament was inspired by some interpretations of quilt blocks done in cloisonné. I really liked the contrast between the clear colors of the enamel and the gold outline of each area. I also thought that this idea would make a great Christmas ornament. The metallic outline of the quilt pieces and the block as a whole will look good twinkling on a tree.

If you prefer not to do the ornament on Plastic Canvas, it could also be done on 14-mesh needlepoint canvas, or as a cross-stitch ornament.

Materials

14 mesh plastic canvas in clear, white or ivory
1 spool Kreinik #16 (medium) braid in 002HL
1 skein each DMC floss in 340, 776, 825, and 996

You could also make the metallic outline stand out more by using another brighter color of gold, like 202HL. Since a relatively small amount of floss is used, you could also use colors from your stash.

Step-by-step Instructions

Begin stitching by completing all the inner outlines of the patches, according to the graph on the next page. At this point do NOT stitch the outer border, as this will serve as the final outline to join the front and back of the ornament.

Now begin filling in the patches with your floss. 825 is the color I used for the rectangular patches (navy on the graph). I stitched these first to give me something for anchoring.

Then I filled in the square patches, first 776 (pink on the graph), next 996 (light blue on the graph). Finally I filled in the 340 periwinkle blue squares (violet on the graph).

Repeat in a different part of the canvas if you want your ornament to be finished front and back. Cut out the finished stitching, leaving 1 hole of canvas all around for finishing.

If you did not stitch a back, cut out another piece of plastic canvas the same size. Also cut a piece of gold braid about 3-4 inches long, double this and knot it to be the loop to hang the ornament.

Place the loop between the two pieces of canvas, wrong sides together, at one of the corners. Beginning at this corner, stitch around the edge of the ornament, just as if you were doing regular needlepoint, binding the front and the back to each other.

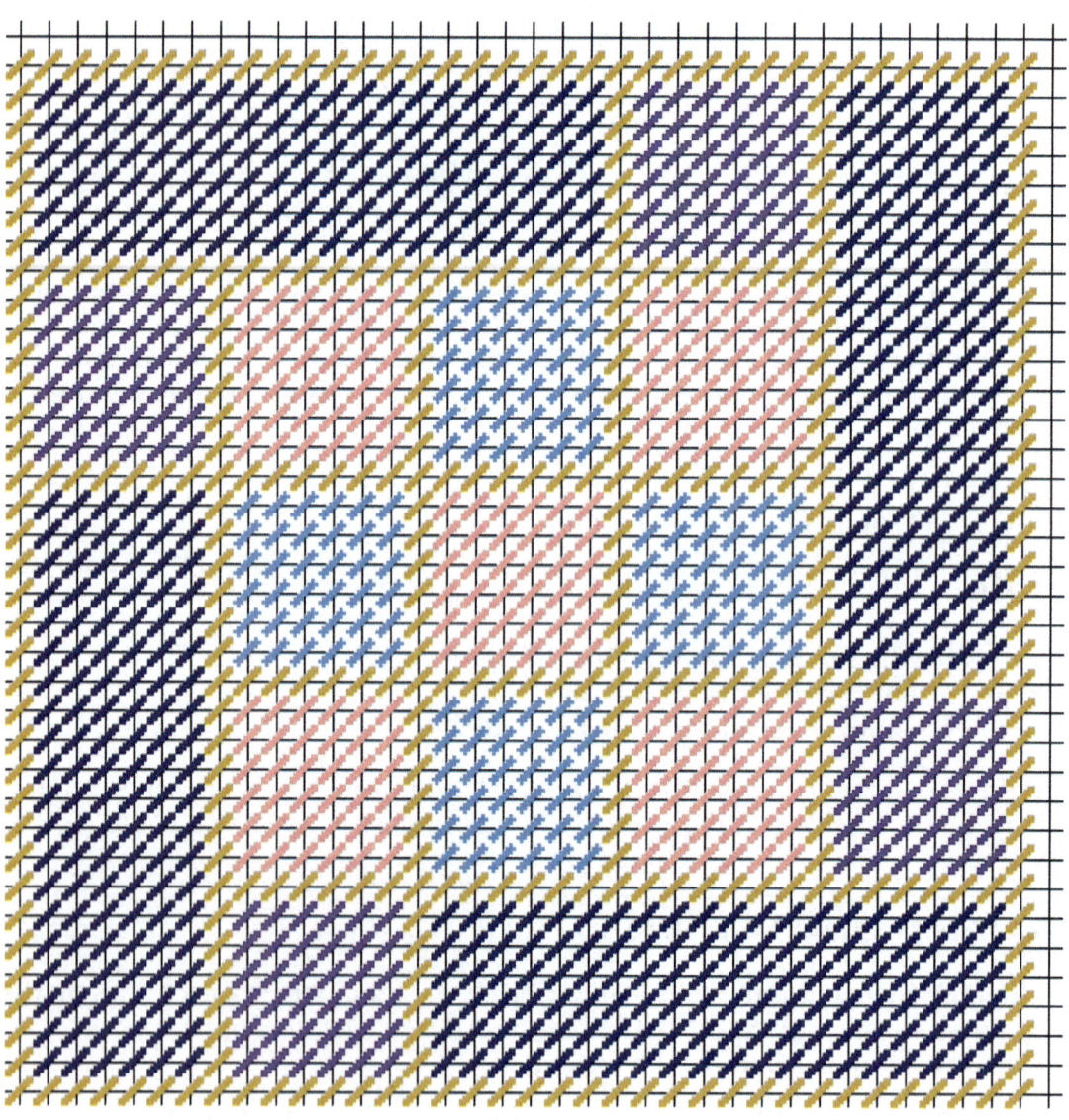

Amish Double Four Patch

Growing up in Pennsylvania, I have a deep love for traditional Amish quilts. They use only solid colors in a limited color palette of black, red, violet, blue, and green; the same colors you see in their clothes. Without prints, the quilts take on a wonderful geometric look as you can see in this project. The simple stitches make it a great choice for beginners.

Materials

5 colors silk or silk/wool blend, avoid yellow, orange, and white
7x 8 inch piece of 18-mesh mono canvas

Step-by-step Instructions

Stitch the project using the chart on page 18. The inner border and the small solid blocks are stitched using the same color of thread in the model. Another possibility is to make the large squares and inner border match. You could also use two different colors or one of the colors in the smaller blocks. It's your project; pick the colors you want.

18

The small solid blocks are **Mosaic,** below left. The large solid blocks are **Scotch Stitch,** below center. The sides of the inner border are **Diagonal Gobelin,** below right. Amish quilts often use corner blocks as you see here. In the model and the chart they are stitched in the border color.

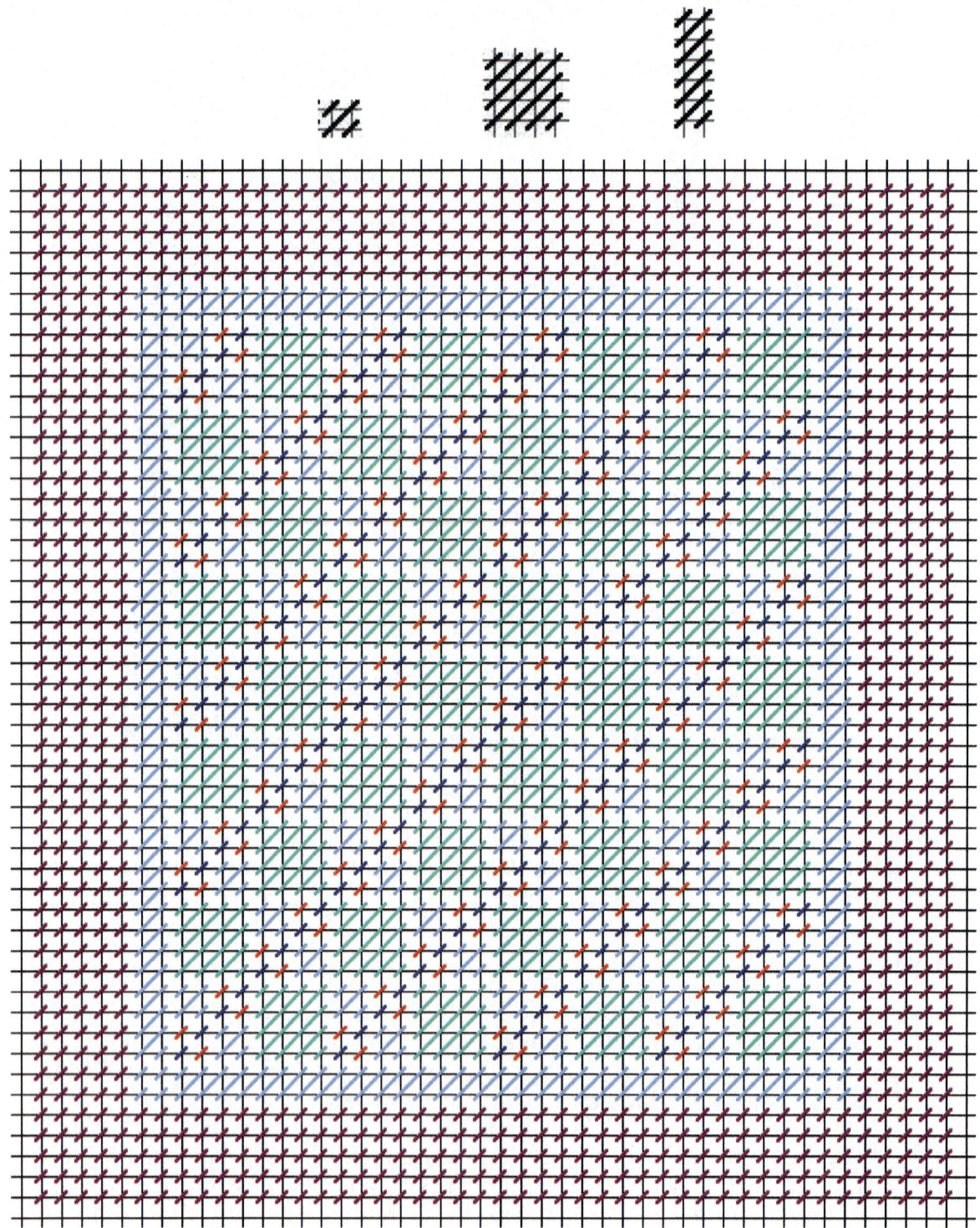

Holiday Rickrack Mini-sock

    Bright with traditional colors and using a classic one-patch quilt pattern, the Holiday Rickrack Mini-sock will only take an evening or two to stitch and will create a lovely addition to your Christmas decor.

    During the 1930's many people made quilts from feedsacks using a single patch. It was a very thrifty way to use up feedsacks and scraps of fabric. Along with hexagonal shapes, half-square triangles, and squares, equilateral triangles were popular for this.

    The combination of alternating triangles reminded me of rickrack and I thought stitching it in an overdyed thread would make it more festive.

    The Holiday Rickrack Mini-sock takes advantage of the fact that rickrack trim looks like two rows of triangles back-to-back. This was a popular Depression pattern, not only because it was thrifty, but also because rickrack was a popular and inexpensive trim on household linens and clothing.

If you don't want to use a holiday theme, pick an overdye you like. Make the rickrack from it and choose a coordinating background color. It can be made so quickly, you can easily make a bunch.

Materials

Cream or white metallic with wool or silk, such as Silk Lame
   (model uses Wool Crepe from Amy's – no longer made)
1 skein Holiday Watercolours
8×10 inch piece 18-mesh white mono canvas

Step-by-step Instructions

Using a permanent dye-based marker (like Pigma Microns or Copic markers) trace the outline of the mini-sock onto your canvas, page 22.

The entire stocking is stitched in Trianglepoint compound triangles. You can vary the size of these triangles by varying the number of stitches in them. The picture below shows the different sizes of triangles.

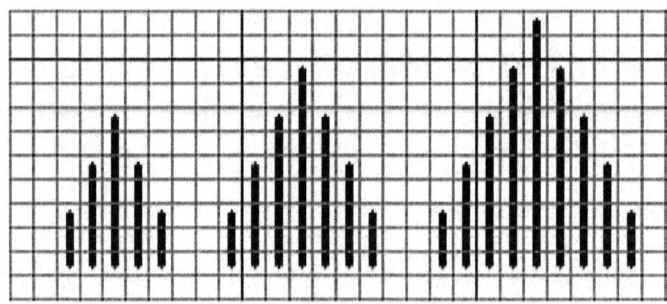

Begin stitching in the top center of the outline with the top of a Watercolours triangle, diagrammed below, using on strand of Watercolours. Make one of these triangles and fill out the row on either side with more of the Watercolours triangles.

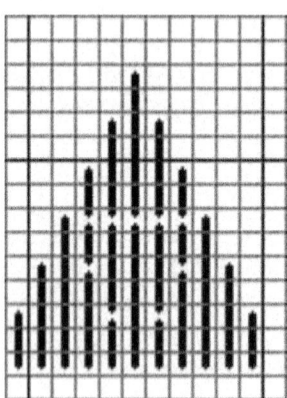

Fill up the spaces with triangles in the background thread. This will complete the top row.

The second row is essentially and upside down version of the top row. The colored triangles are centered under the longest stitch of the background triangles. This is what creates the rickrack effect.

Continue stitching in this manner until the outline is filled. I stitched the Watercolours triangles first for each pair of rows and then filled in the background.

Making the Pattern Larger

If you want to make this pattern on a larger scale, you must continue to have large triangles made up of only six small triangles (bottom row of three triangles). Thus to increase the size of the triangles, you must make each individual small triangle larger. To do this, increase the number of stitches (and their length) in each small triangle. These triangles can be 2-4-6-4-2. Larger triangles could be 2-4-6-8-6-4-2 or 2-4-6-8-10-8-6-4-2. You'll find diagrams of these bigger triangles on the previous page.

22

Mini-sock Outline

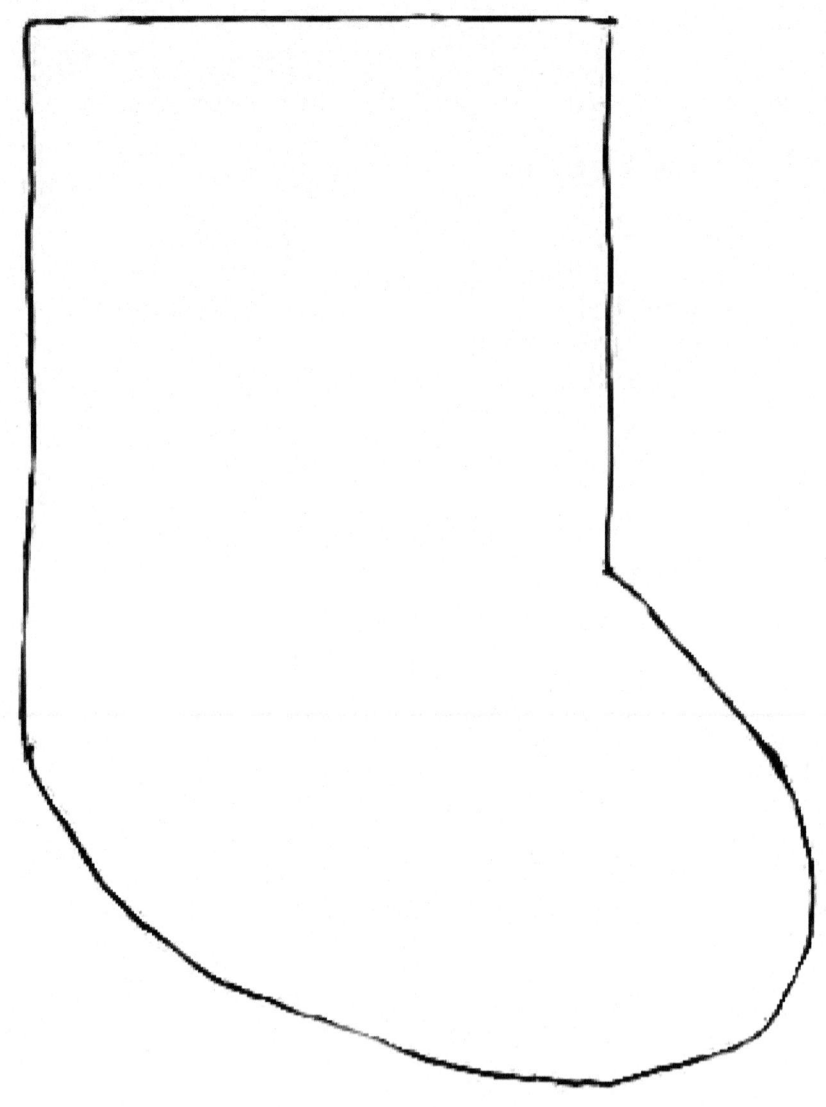

Autumn Leaf Diamond

This project is designed to use up leftover threads. It's easy to vary the look of the project by changing the color used for the leaves. The variegated thread used for the middle border can match or coordinate with the leaf color.

Materials

    7 inch square of 14-mesh needlepoint canvas
    4 colors of leftover knitting yarn, or thread as follows
        1 leafy color (yellow in model)
        1 background color (cream in model)
        1 multi-colored that has the leaf color in it (middle border in model)
        1 accent color that is in multi-color (green in model)

Please note: If you have friends who stitch the chances are that they might have some canvas to give to you. In addition, needlepoint shops often have small bits of canvas leftover from other pieces they sell and sell them at a discount. I always keep a bunch of mine for these leftover projects.

The knitting yarn you pick should be about sock weight and should be even in width. Needlepoint is not the technique for nubby yarns. Many knitting yarns have more than one strand in them and can be thinned by pulling out one or more strands.

You will need 4 yards of yellow and green, about 1-2 of cream, and 2 of multi-color.

Step-by-step Instructions

Start by finding the center hole and stitch the "stem" of the leaf. Complete stitching that one leaf and its background. Use the chart on the next page to stitch.

Go back to the center and stitch a second leaf. You'll notice that where two leaves meet the stitches make a right angle. You'll also note that each leaf is made of a bunch of diamonds and partial diamonds. These stitches mimic the patches of the quilt on which this ornament is based.

Once you have stitched the center section, stitch the borders. There are three of them and they go all the way around the ornament.

When you have completed the ornament, cut it out five threads beyond each of the points of the diamond, making a big square, with the diamond almost touching the middle point of each side.

Turn under that five stitch margin to make a clean edge and fold those unstitched corners to the back. Now the stitching is on the front and the unstitched canvas is on the back.

Take a loop of ribbon to be a hanger and tuck it between the stitching and the folded canvas at one of the corners.

Bring two of the folded corners to meet each other and stitch them together by bringing the needle out of the canvas on one side of the seam and back into the canvas on the other side of the seam. Go back and cross over the stitches you have already made.

Do this for each corner, until the ornament is stitched together. Take some felt and trace the ornament on it. Cut out the felt about 1/8" smaller all around and glue it to the back of the ornament.

Sunburst

This ornament is based on a variation of the Log Cabin quilt block. It has a "scrappy" look, using different threads from my stash for each bar.

The design is easy to vary. If you make it from all Scotch Stitches instead, the ornament will be larger. You can make the design more dramatic by making the three borders a different color instead of shades of the background color. Think about making it a perfect size to fit into self-finishing coasters. If you made four in different colors, it would be a fantastic gift.

Changing the threads you use can also affect the finished look of the design. I love projects like this as a way to use up threads from my stash. The model uses stash threads, not in color families.

Materials

6 inch square 18-mesh mono needlepoint canvas
1 skein thread in background color
6-12 threads in one color family (family #1)
6-12 threads in a second color family (family #2)

Step-by-step Instructions

Begin in the middle of the ornament and stitch the **Mosaics** charted in yellow and olive on the chart on the next page using the lightest shade in color family #1 or two scrap threads. Notice that the stitches at the end of each arm are **Half Mosaics.** The direction of these stitches determines whether the Mosaics in the arm are **Reverse Mosaics.**

Stitch the Mosaics charted in orange and fuchsia using the medium shade in color family #1 or two scrap threads.

Stitch the Mosaics charted in burgundy and red using the dark shade in color family #1 or two scrap threads.

Begin to stitch the background by stitching the square background areas, charted in periwinkle blue, using the pale shade in color family #2. All of these stitches are Mosaics or Reverse Mosaics; there are no Half Mosaics in these areas.

Stitch the inside border, charted in aqua using the light shade in color family #2. The stitches in all the borders will change direction as they go around the ornaments.

Stitch the middle border, charted in blue, using the medium shade in color family #2.

Stitch the outer border, charted in black, using the dark shade in color family #2.

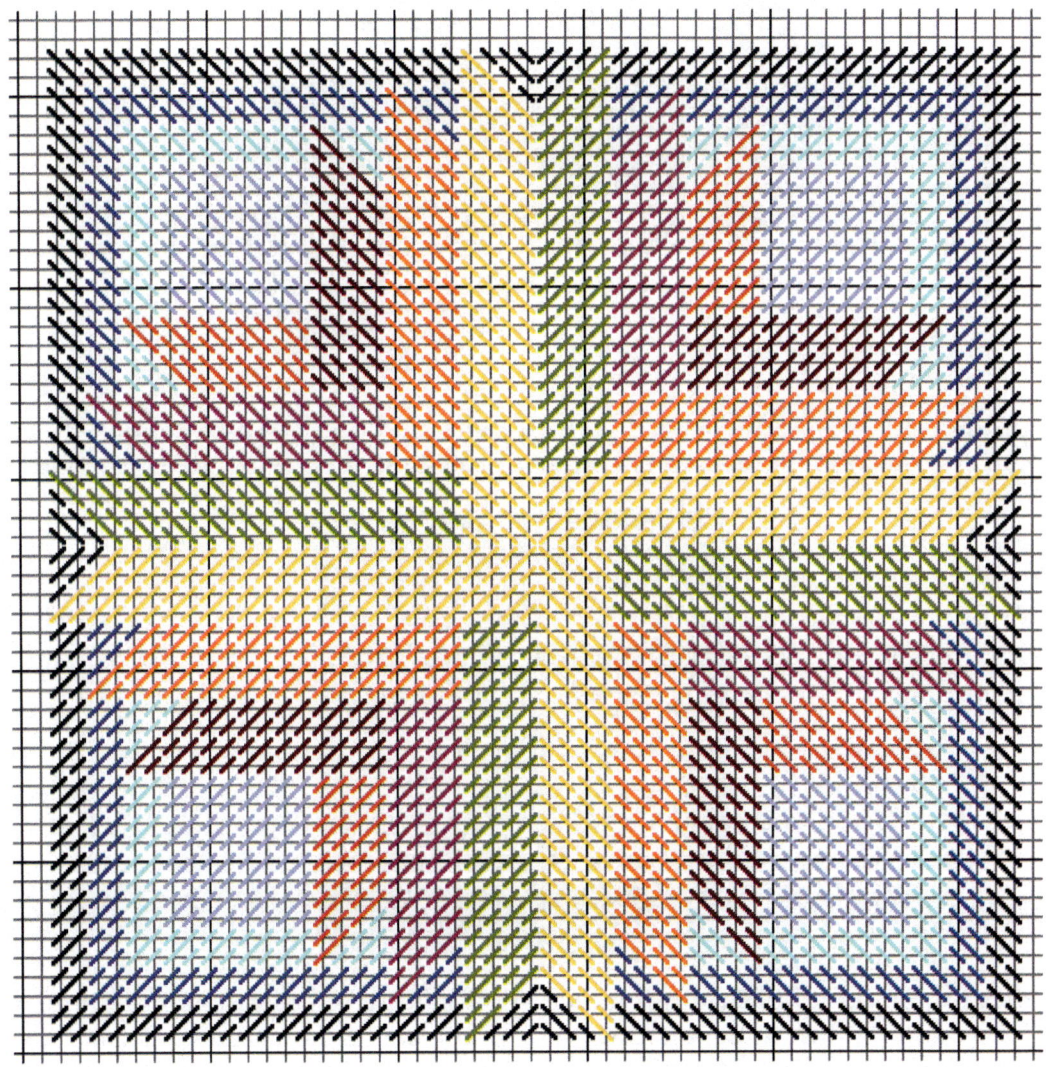

Amish Bargello Mini-sock

My inspiration for this mini-sock came from a simple Bargello quilt, below, that was done in traditional Amish colors. The colors from the quilt's borders form the top of the sock.

The pattern in the center of the quilt makes up the body of the stocking. I lightened the blue of the inner border and the matching color in the center for more contrast. I also used fewer colors in keeping with the smaller size of the needlepoint.

Materials

8x10 inch piece 18-mesh mono canvas
9 shades of wool, matte silk, or matte silk/wool blend (see note)

PLEASE NOTE: A more difficult task in converting the quilt to needlepoint is the color adaptation. The quilt has a sequence of thirteen colors. That's fine for something large but won't work well on a small mini-sock. I cut down the number of colors to nine, with dark gray, coral, red, lavender, violet, medium and medium-dark green, medium light blue, and blue. I also liked the wide border so I added a cuff in navy with a medium light blue border.

Step-by-step Instructions

Using a permanent dye-based marker (like Pigma Microns or Copic markers) trace the outline of the mini-sock onto your canvas, page 30.

Draw a line across the top about 3/4" down for the cuff. The cuff would be a richer blue if it was colored with a navy pen at this point. This will also disguise any white canvas that might show through.

Stitch a dark gray row somewhere near the center, using the line below. Begin with the block of 6 stitches in the very center of the line. Stitch out to either end.

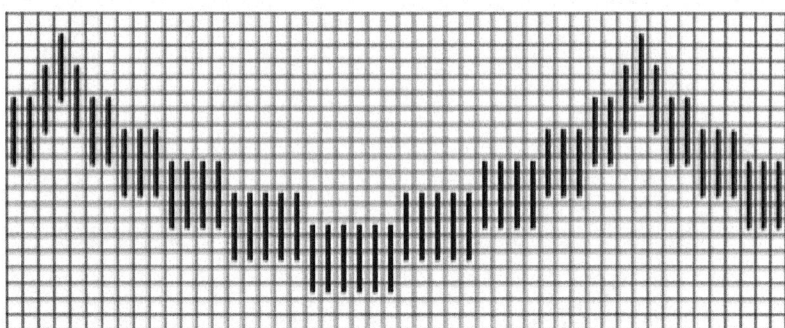

Following a color sequence you like, stitch the body of the mini-sock. At the lie you drew for the cuff, stitch a row of **Upright Gobelin** over four threads, below. Fill in the top of the stocking with the same Bargello line using the navy thread.

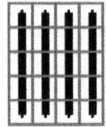

Mini-sock Outline

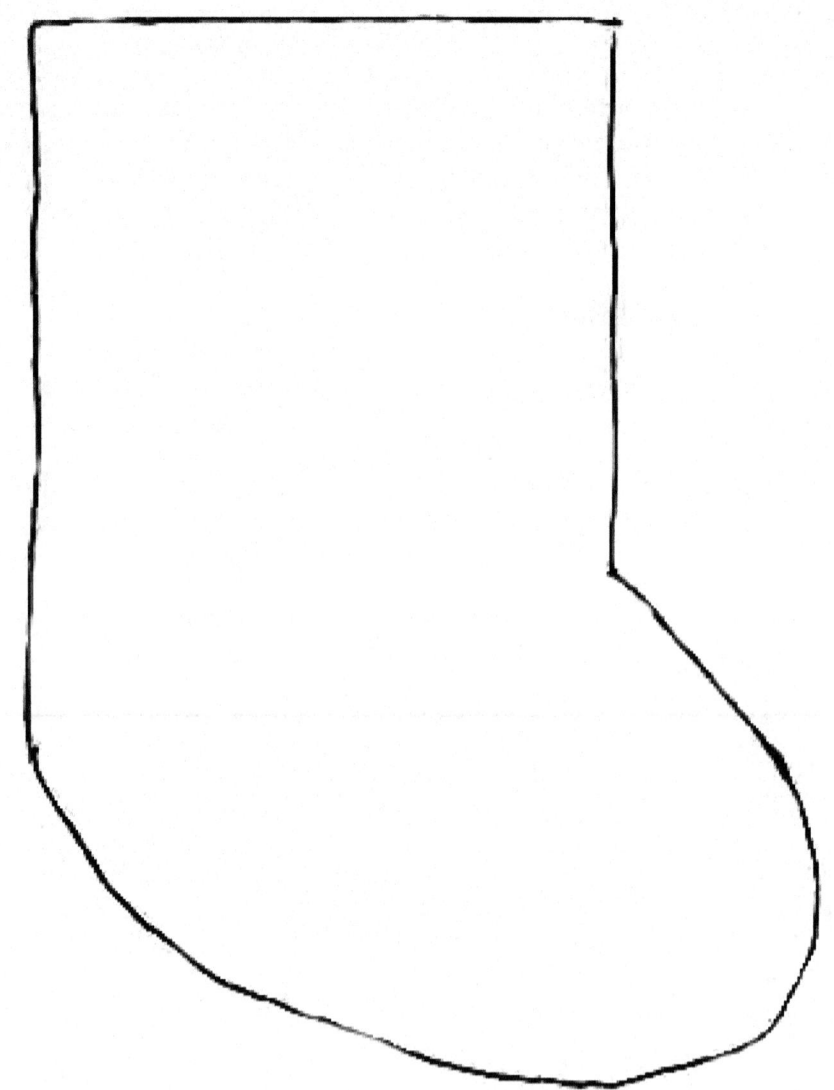

Scrappy Squares

This design is based on a quilt made up of squares that are multiples of each other. That's easy to do in needlepoint with Box Stitches. A Mosaic Stitch is twice the size of a Tent Stitch. A Scotch Stitch over 4 threads is twice the size if a Mosaic Stitch. A bigger Scotch (or in this case a Mosaic in a Diagonal Gobelin border) is twice the size of the Scotch.

Knowing this you can mix and match squares to create a lively design.

This quilt uses all solid colors. If you chose to use hand-dyes, as I did, you will mimic the slightly shaded look of batik quilting fabrics.

Materials

5×7 inch piece 18-mesh mono canvas
at least 12 colors of solid or hand-dyed threads
metallic thread in an accent color (optional)
border color (optional)

Most of the threads used were Dinky Dyes stranded silk. A few colors of Grandeur were used, and white Crystal Braid was the accent thread.

Step-by-step Instructions

The design is 32 stitches wide and 48 stitches tall without the border. To make it fit into a 2"x3" frame add a row of Tent in the metallic at the top and bottom and a two row border of Diagonal Gobelin around the entire piece. Although you can chose to use one of the main colors for the border, another color could be used that does not appear in the quilt.

Your choice for what color should go in each square should be picked at random from among your palette of colors. Just don't put the same or similar colors next to each other.

Instead of a complete diagram of the quilt you'll find a map below. Folks who quilt are quite familiar with these kinds of diagrams. They show the individual patches or blocks in solid colors. A single square on this map is a Mosaic Stitch. Most groupings of four squares of the same color are Scotch Stitches over four threads. Among these there are a few blocks of four Mosaic Stitches in the same color (you can see these in the finished stitching). Sixteen blocks together in the same color are the Mosaic-Diagonal Gobelin Blocks.

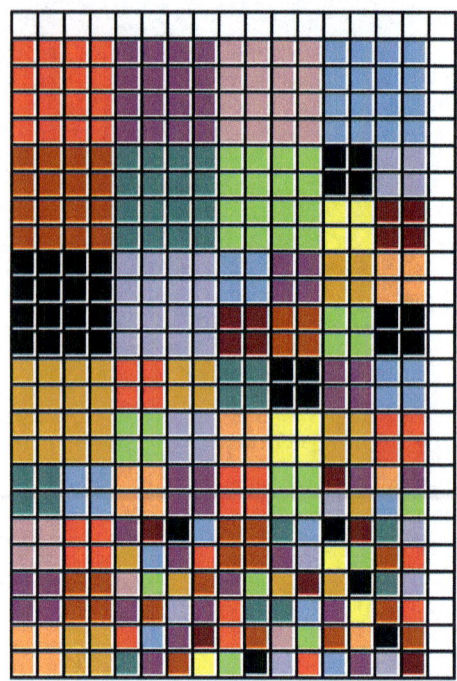

The original quilt had very simple stitching and quilting which is why these stitches are flat. If you'd like more texture or variety you can substitute other stitches covering the same area.

Tulips

This cheerful quilt is one of many quilt blocks from the Great Depression. These quilts often have this scrappy look because they are made from leftover fabric and from the printed fabric that was used to make feedsacks. The bright colors are also typical of these quilts.

Materials

5x7 inch 18-mesh mono needlepoint canvas
35-70 threads in various colors
1 skein background thread

Step-by-step Instructions

The project has seven rows of five tulips. A single tulip block is charted on the next page and will be repeated for all the tulips. It's easiest to stitch all the tulips first and then to fill in the background.

Depending on your canvas color, you may skip the background. This will create a contrast between the patchy tulips and the solid background. I preferred the patchy look of the stitched background.

The block is stitched as charted below in a combination of **Scotch** and **Half-scotch** in regular and reverse orientation.

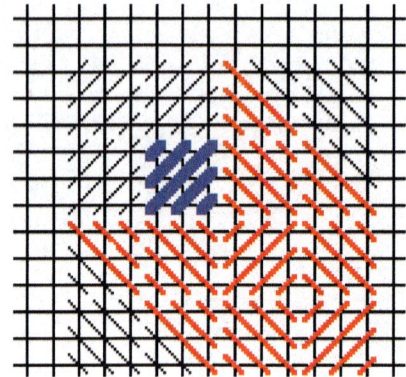

Rhodes Heart

Inspired by a heart quilt, this Rhodes Stitch heart uses many threads in the same color (I used red) to create a great stash-buster project.

It uses only one stitch, Rhodes, which you can make any size you like. Pick the mesh you like to make it big or small. The model is stitched on 18-mesh mono and is about 5×4, perfect for a box top.

Materials

8x9 inch piece 18-mesh mono canvas
20 or more threads in the same color

Step-by-step Instructions

Rhodes Stitch was invented by and named for the great British stitcher, Mary Rhodes. To create the stitch you will cross the front diagonally moving either clockwise or counter-clockwise until you get back to the starting point. This creates a lovely swirling effect.

Rhodes Stitch can be made any size and shape. Mine are square and go over 5 threads. Counterclockwise is shown next page top. Clockwise is shown next page bottom. Start stitching at the arrow.

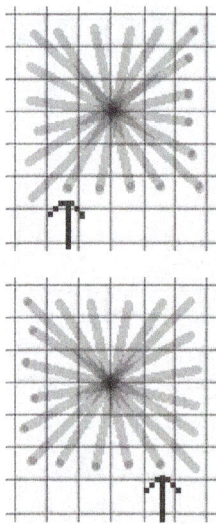

It's important in making this stitch that you always go in the same direction to make the stitch and that you always start at the same point on the outside. That keeps the stitches consistent and maximizes their impact.

This stitch also looks best if the top stitch for each unit is on the true diagonal. To achieve this always start your stitch one thread after a corner.

Your project will look beautifully random if you don't put stitches using similar colors or threads next to each other.

Start stitching at the bottom and literally pick threads at random from your project bag. If the thread you pick is too similar, set it aside and pick another thread. Follow the plan below for placement

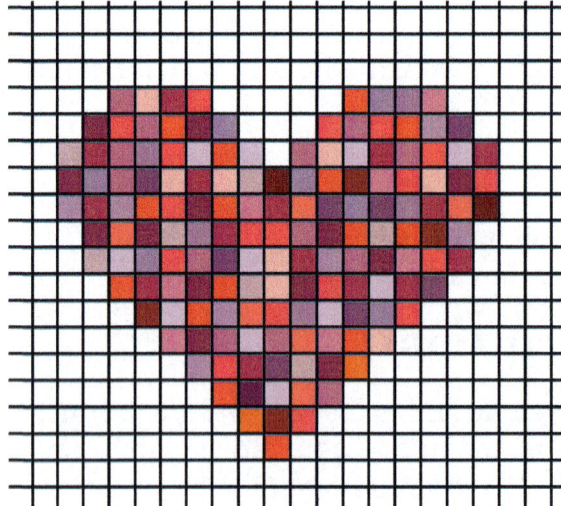

It's amazing how a single stitch and leftover threads can combine to make something great!

Wedding Day

This charming pattern is a great way to use up those bits and pieces of threads while stitching something that's great for a boxtop or to put inside a Sudberry trivet.

The quilt block is called Wedding Day. It features a light blue background, stitched here in two similar colors of crewel wool. Cream or white diamonds and smaller diamonds stitched from scrap threads create the pattern.

Materials

1 cream or white single-strand thread (model used Ty-Di Just Cotton - no longer made)
2 colors crewel wool in background color, close but not matching (model uses Sanjou and Valdani crewel wool)
10 inch square 18-mesh mono canvas
25 or more scraps of thread from your stash

Use two colors of crewel for the background to give the feel of a print. While in a quilt the background would be solid and the scrap squares prints, the colored squares are just too small to show variation in color without wasting thread. By using two different threads in the background, you'll keep the quilt portrait from being dull.

Step-by-step Instructions

The setting of the quilt is three blocks in each direction. On 18-mesh canvas, the finished size is about 5.5" square. To make it larger, add borders or additional blocks.

Stitch each block following the chart below.

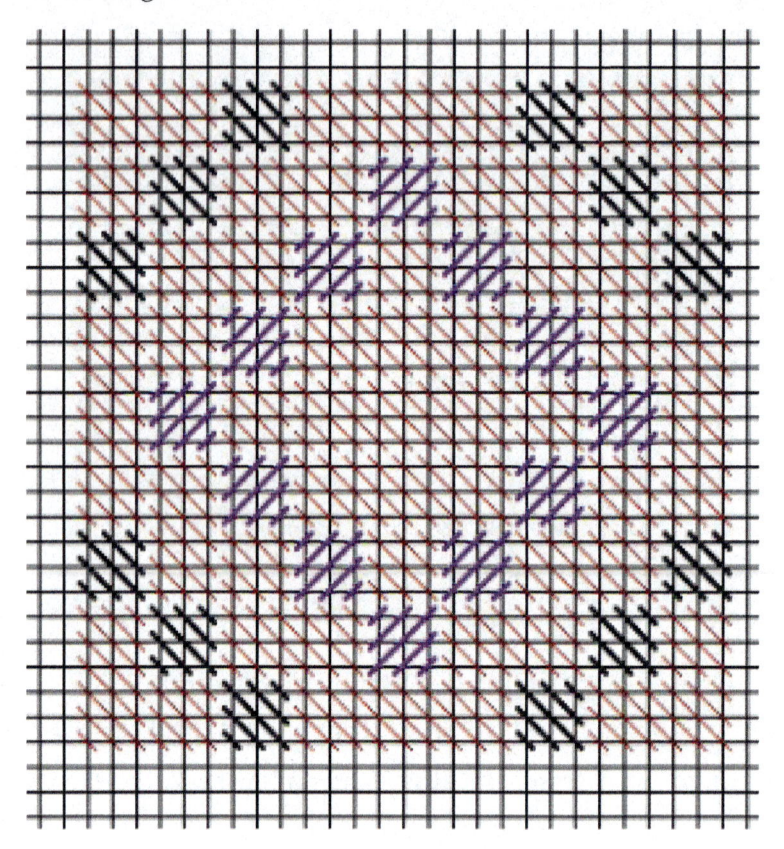

Scrap Basket

This flexible project uses any square stitch to make a charming woven design. The project creates a quilt that is 17 units by 21 units, but it can be expanded to any size you like. I used small Scotch Stitches as my square stitch, but you could use larger Scotch Stitches in the size of your choice.

The colored areas of the quilt are made of rows of three units. The direction of the units alternates, giving the lines a woven look. This look is muted by the changing colors of the scrap quilt.

You can also make a couple of cool variations:

* Make the colored rectangles stand out more by making them in a square cross stitch, such as Smyrna Cross or Rice.
* Turn it into a quilt that looks like a real basket by using two closely related shades, one for each direction of lines and a much darker shade of the same color for the background.

Materials

7×8 inch piece mono 18-mesh needlepoint canvas
1 skein background thread
up to 98 assorted scrap threads in colors, textures, and fibers of your choice

Step-by-step Instructions

The pattern, below, is a map of the design. Because you chose the square stitch you will use for the project, this map just shows the layout. Colored squares are made using your scrap threads. White squares are background.

I found it easiest to stitch a bunch of the scrap units, then fill in the background.

Because the scrap rectangles are small, this is a great project for your smaller bits of thread. But this also shows up a problem that can occur in these projects. If the colors of threads in adjacent areas are too close in color, your design will have visual "holes." There are a couple of these here.

Avoid this problem by keeping the colors in adjacent areas different. Work to scatter attention-getting threads, such as metallics, around the design. You can see how this works in the picture of the model.

Bookshelf

    This project is a very quick and easy quilt design – the bookshelf quilt. It's great for using little bits of thread. Although mine is small, you can easily expand it or stitch it on larger mesh canvases. While I have seen very large bookshelf quilts, the delicacy of this design on 18-mesh canvas makes smaller sizes best. If you want a large design choose a larger mesh canvas. I finished it in a Planet Earth luggage tag.

    Somebody got a very clever idea for using long skinny pieces of fabric leftover from making quilts. Every quiltmaker has them because you are supposed to cut off the selvedge plus an inch or so on either edge of your fabric. The edges are woven more tightly to keep the fabric from raveling.

    What can you do with a bunch of strips about an inch wide and all different lengths?

    They look like books. So why not make a quilt of a bookshelf? The colors you use won't matter nor will the length because books come in all sorts of sizes and colors. All you need to add is the fabric to be the back of the bookshelf and the bookshelf quilt was born.

    Most of the ones I have seen are pretty large, but they can be made any size, just the way real bookshelves are made. I'm sure you could make a bookshelf quilt with the colors arranged beautifully to blend into each other but I like the same random assortment of color that real bookshelves have.

Materials

1 skein white thread of your choice (model uses Vineyard Merino)
40-50 assorted scrap threads 12" or more
7 inch square 18-mesh mono canvas

I used lots of non-metallic threads from my scrap bag. Any non-metallic thread will work. Depending on the length of your thread you will be able to make one or more books.

Step-by-step Instructions

The quilt fits into a 2.5x3 luggage tag, a size that can also be used for wallets, mini frames, and credit card cases. I chose to have four bookshelves 45 threads wide. To get the proper length the shelves are 15 threads high on top and bottom and 13 threads high in the middle for a total length of 56 threads.

The books and the open shelves above them are stitched in random widths of **Tent** and **Diagonal Gobelin.** Reverse directions of these stitches are also used. The books range from one to four threads wide. Diagrams for all the Gobelin Stitches are below.

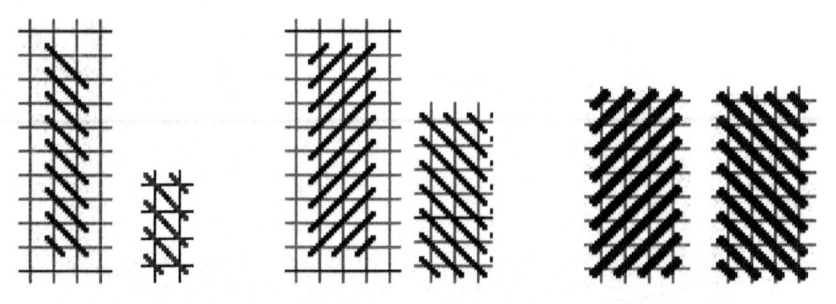

Begin by stitching the upper edge of the top shelf. Mix up the different widths of the stitch and make them different lengths. Be sure to alternate the direction of the stitch with each "book;" this will make the next step easier.

Count down 13 threads from the bottom of this row. This is the bottom of the second row. Make books and the area above the books for this row exactly the same way mixing up widths and lengths and alternating directions.

Count down 13 rows and stitch the third shelf. Once that is complete, count down 15 threads and stitch the top of the bottom shelf.

It's fine to have two or more books the same width and the same color. Books that come in sets would be like this; often books from the same publisher are also like this. I have a set of books on the top shelf.

With the top areas complete, it's easy to fill in the books. Pick a thread at random and stitch one of the books, filling in the area from the bottom of that shelf to the top of the shelf below. You will use the same stitch as used for this top of the shelf.

Once you have one book stitched, if you have enough thread for additional books in the same thread, move to a different area in another row and stitch a second book. Continue in this way until you reach the end of the thread.

Repeat this process with additional threads until all the books are stitched.

Tips for Success: Most bookshelves have books in different colors. When you stitch strive to keep books in similar colors from being next to each other. It isn't entirely necessary, as it is on many other designs, but your shelf will look better if matching books are the minority.

This design has a messy back. It will always have this if you move threads from row to row. If you want your back to be neat, end each thread after one book is stitched and complete one shelf before moving on to the next.

Jonquil

    This design uses a quilt block type that has been around for a long time, but is only called "half-square triangles" recently. Quilts based on these right triangles are very popular. It's a specific way of making triangles that's very easy for the quilter to do. It is also an easy and flexible basis for needlepoint quilt portraits.

The quilt is based on a crib quilt that had an offset center of square rings in two alternating colors plus a background. Thinking of my yard in spring, I made it in the colors of daffodils, one of my favorite flowers. If you think of them as only being "daffodil yellow," look at some bulb catalogs. You'll see they come in many different styles and in a broad range of yellows, plus some oranges and whites, I used flower colors and leaf colors as the basis for my hollow squares.

To find my colors I pulled out as many threads as I could find in yellow, light shades of green (especially yellow green), and a few oranges. The threads were picked at random for the colored triangles. My biggest concern was to keep colors that were similar away from each other.

Materials

1 skein Watercolours 312 Linen (white, cream and blue)
assorted threads in yellow, orange, green, and light yellow-green
7x8 inch piece 18-mesh mono needlepoint canvas

Because this project is based of a type of flower, you can substitute the yellow and orange threads for threads the color of any flower you like. If the flower of your choice is white, however, you will need to change the background color to something dark, such as navy, dark grey, or black.

PLEASE NOTE: This project looks cleanest when the background is white. But any thread can be used. This color of Watercolours was used in the model.

The Half-square Triangle

If you take a square and cut it diagonally down the middle (i.e. from corner to corner) you will get two equal right triangles. In quilting these are called "half-square triangles" because that is how they are cut out. Put two of them together and you get a square. Put various combinations of squares and these triangles together and you get bigger triangles. There are lots of quilts and quilt blocks out there that use this basic piece.

In needlepoint we have squares too. We call them Scotch and Mosaic Stitches. So, half-square triangle quilts should be as easy to translate to needlepoint as quilts made up only of squares.

It ends up being slightly more difficult because our squares always have a stitch running right along that corner-to-corner cut, below. That means you cannot in needlepoint create two equal half-square triangles; one of the triangles will have to contain the long corner-to-corner stitch.

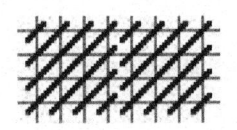

Therefore if you have a 4x4 Scotch Stitch for example, you will have one side that has four stitches, next page left, and one with only three, next page right.

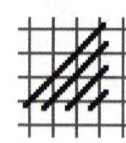

Once you know this trick it's easy to split the blocks. It's also easy to change slants to fit changing directions in the quilt. This quilt portrait, below, from my book *Color through the Ages,* is an example of a half-square triangle piece that does this.

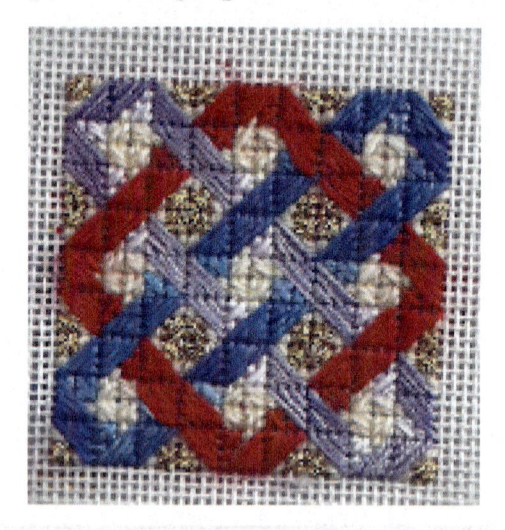

The next question is where to put the bigger block. It should always be included in the main part of the design, not the background. Once you know how to split the blocks and where to put the bigger triangle, these quilts become easy to reproduce.

Step-by-step Instructions

This quilt uses two stitches in oriented to be the top or bottom half of the square with stitches in either direction (normal and reverse), depending on the direction of the triangle and the quadrant it is in. A combination of one of each stitch makes a complete square block, although this structure is hidden because of the color changes.

All background triangles are stitched in **Scotch-half-scotch Triangles**, below left, and **Reverse Scotch-half-scotch Triangles**, below right, using one strand of Watercolours or your background thread.

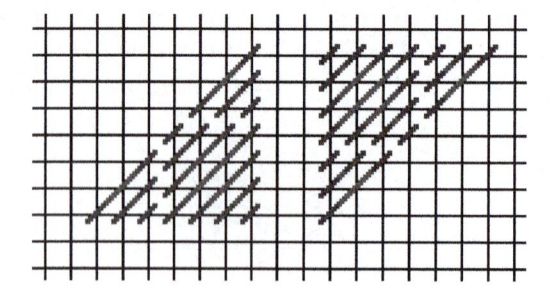

All colored triangles are stitched in **Half Speyside,** below top, or **Reverse Half Speyside,** below bottom, using yellow, orange, or green threads from your stash.

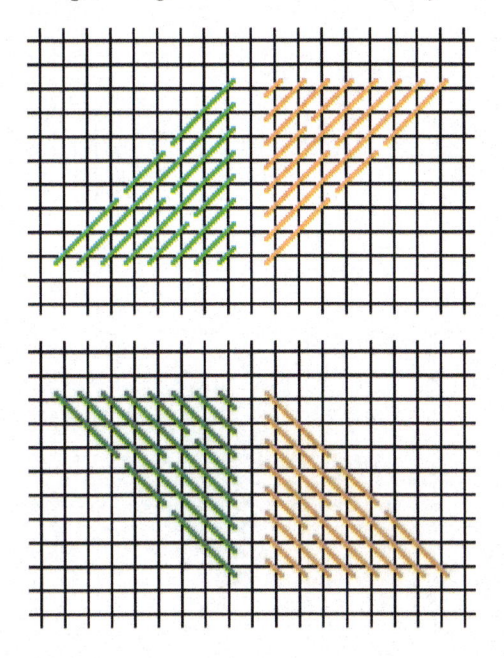

You will be making concentric diamonds following the chart, page 48. Beginning with the small background diamond, the rings are:
* Background
* Yellow
* Background
* Green
* Background
* Yellow
* Background
* Green
* Background
* Yellow
* Background
* Green
* Background
* Yellow

Begin stitching the "center" diamond 1.5" up and .75" in from where you want the corner of the project to be. Stitch one round at a time. Notice that the triangles in each round use the same stitch and its reverse. A combination of one of each stitch makes a complete square block.

As you stitch parts of the round will drop out because the center is offset. The project picture on page 44 and the chart, next page, both show you how this occurs.

48

Preppy Heart

49

This project is based on a quilt I saw in *Modern Quilting*. The structure of the blocks, half-square triangles, and the color scheme, complementary, are familiar. The background and the borders are less familiar, however. They give us two great ways to create dynamic needlepoint easily that can be transferred to many other projects.

Materials

1 card or skein light pink (model uses Pebbly Perle - no longer made)
1 skein white solid or semi-solid thread
assorted threads in white pink, and lime green
7 inch square pink 18-mesh mono canvas

Step-by-step Instructions

The heart is made up of Scotch Stitches over four threads divided in two. The overall size of the heart is twelve blocks wide by eleven blocks high or 48 x 44 stitches. The map below shows the layout of the quilt.

Half-Scotch triangles are not divided evenly. The longest stitch in each square is made in the dominant color. That triangle is diagrammed below. The left side of the quilt is **Reverse Scotch.** The right side is **Scotch.**

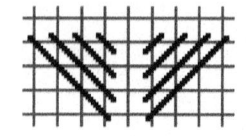

The majority of blocks have white as the smaller triangle's color. A few have white as the dominant color. The other color in each block is randomly picked between the two complements. Very occasionally a white/white block is made.

To make the quilt I stitched all the white triangles first. Then I used one thread at a time to fill in the blocks. I scattered each thread around the heart, keeping adjacent squares from having the same dominant thread.

Add the background to the design once it is completely stitched. The heart should be centered in the area. It can be any size you like. The model has eleven threads of background at the narrowest point on all sides. It is stitched in **T Stitch,** next page.

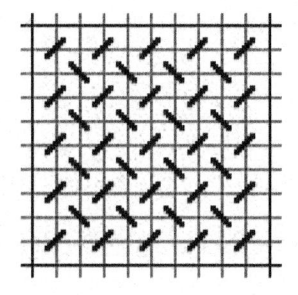

Once the background is stitched, stitch the border in **Upright Gobelin over 4 Threads**, below left. Remember that the corners are mitered when making this stitch, below right. It is stitched with random lengths of pink and green thread, alternating the colors. Remember not to split the mitered part of the corner between two colors; that would cause the corner to attract too much attention.

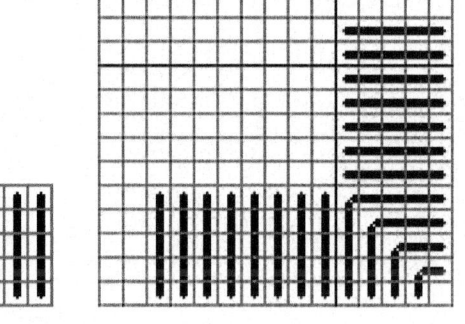

Adding Texture not Color

If you have spent much time looking at quilts you have probably been impressed by ones where the patchwork is accompanied by large areas of "background," often elaborately quilted. The interesting thing about these designs is that the quilting adds texture but doesn't add color because the quilting thread is the same color as the fabric, which is a solid color.

This effect is not hard to replicate in needlepoint. When we are making needlepoint quilt portraits though, we tend to forget it. That's a shame because it functions the way a great background does for a decorative needlepoint, it sets off the focal point.

If your background color does not match the canvas color you can use any textured stitch or Tent Stitch pattern. Patterns should be made in two threads with contrasting textures but the same color.

If your canvas is colored, you have a wonderful opportunity to add texture by to using some additional techniques. Open stitches can be used, as can Blackwork and darning patterns. You can still use Tent Stitch patterns but you can leave out the background stitches, allowing the bare canvas to be the background.

When your thread is slightly different in color than the bare canvas, it also changes the color. I did that here by using a lighter shade of pink.

Border

I tend to shy away from borders, largely because I am very bad at counting. If I need to count and there is nothing in the design to help me, I'm lost. I think many needlepointers must have the same problem, because borders are not common in needlepoint.

Quilters don't have this problem. In fact multiple borders can often be seen on quilts. For me translating borders to needlepoint is not easy because of the counting problem. That's why I love this unusual border. I saw it years ago and cut out the picture for my idea notebook. Here it stands on its own, but it also plays nicely with borders in a single color. You can also build up a wider border by making multiples of this border in a narrower stitch.

The stitch used for this border is Upright Gobelin, previous page. This stitch allows you to create straight edges to end each color. Elongated Cashmere Stitches could also be used but only if the corners are lapped instead of mitered.

The key to the look is the random length of each block. You can decide on these lengths as you go, by stitching until you think the block is big enough. You can also decide the length before you stitch s block by cutting the threads in random lengths, differing by a few stitches.

It's simple, you don't have to count, and it's quite unique.

Wild Thing

    This quilt is inspired by a thread from &More called Kokadjo, next page. It's a wool/silk blend with 90% wool and 10% silk. It comes in both solid colors and multi-colors. The multi-color thread I used is bright and has colors you might not put together; it's wild. You'll learn about taming multi-color threads as well as about creating a color scheme based on them.

    I finished it in a Lee eBook cover. If you will be putting your needlepoint into an item that gets lots of wear, chose single-strand threads of a single fiber, such as wool, cotton, silk, or linen.

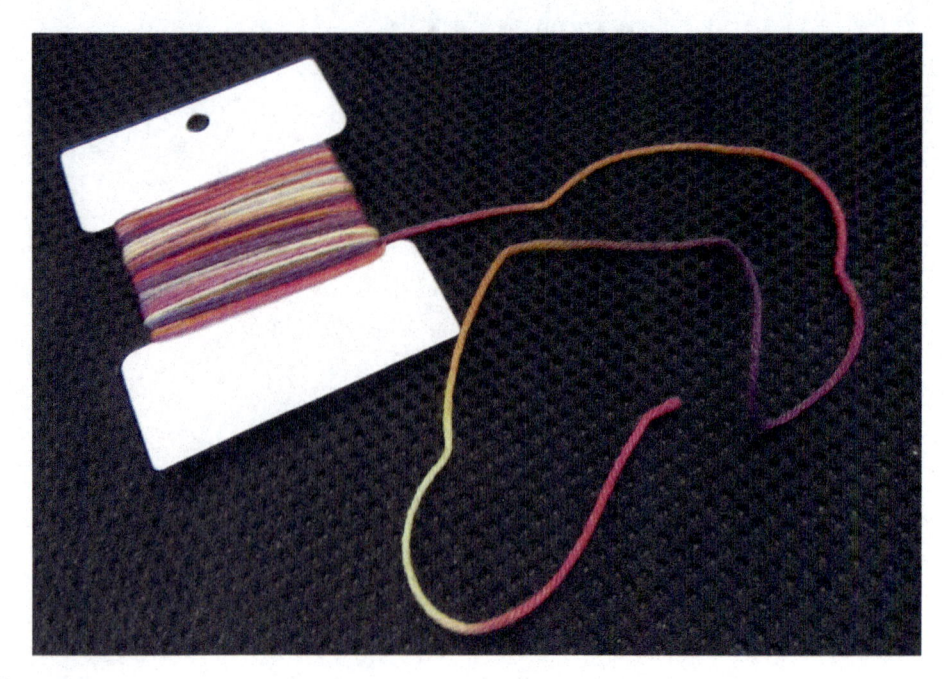

Materials

1 card Kokadjo multi-color thread from &More or other multi-color thread of your choice
9 threads in colors to coordinate with multi-color
1 skein natural or cream thread for background
7x9 inch piece 13-mesh mono canvas

Taming the Wild Thread

When a thread contains several different colors, especially if they are bright, I think of them as wild; they are all over the place. Often, as is the case here, there is no main color. You may have tried threads like this in projects and been unhappy with the results because they just looked confused. That's because we need to add colors and threads to give them the definition they lack.

I think of this process as "taming" the thread. Here are a few ways to do this.

* A great way to do this is to add white, natural, or cream as the background. These light colors tend to soften the bright color, so the contrasts don't seem as large. Black as the background does exactly the opposite. Instead of softening, it highlights the contrast in the multi-color, creating an effect called dazzling. That's one reason why Amish quilts seem to sparkle.
* Add muted versions of your colors to the mix. In this quilt the muted red and dusty rose used in some of the blocks echoed the hot pink in the multi-color but added blocks of quieter, less intense color.
* Isolate the wild color from its surroundings with white. White acts as a buffer between the colors preventing clashes and vibration.
* Use it significantly with a solid accent in the color you want to emphasize. I make lots of small ornaments using overdyed threads. Often they tend to be a bit wild. If I pick

one color to emphasize and then use it consistently and often in the piece, it softens the wild child. You can see this at work in the ornament pictured below.

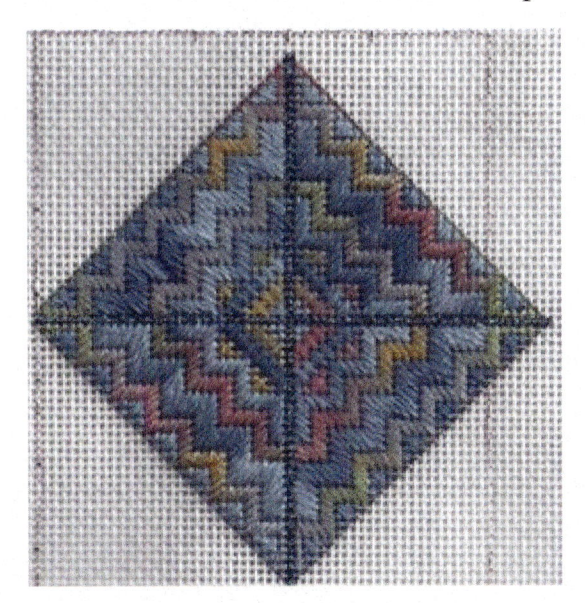

The Caron Collection free design, pictured above, combined the wild overdye with a semi-solid and metallic in blue. It effectively gave the design a focus while still allowing the many colors in the overdye a chance to shine.

Using the Multi-color to Create Palettes

Begin by finding threads to match each of the colors in your wild thread. Depending on your design, you may end up discarding many of them. Let's look at two examples.

First we'll consider the Wild Thing thread. It is a shade called Secret Sunset. It has violet, fuchsia, hot pink, orange, and yellow. If I unwind a bit I see that the color runs are short, 2-3", and there is little transition from color to color. You can see this in the picture on page 54.

To construct my color palette I first found threads that were close matches to the colors in the thread. This gave me violet, orange, and two yellow threads. I then expanded those colors to add an intermediate color, yellow-orange. Brighter than all the other single colors, it adds a pop to those blocks, keeping the eye moving in the design. Even though your palette has a strong color in the multi-color, you want one strong accent to provide balance and contrast within the secondary colors.

I then took one of the colors, hot pink, and expanded it to include four other threads. Dusty Rose takes the color and mutes it significantly. Soft red removes much of the violet in hot pink, darkens the color, and mutes it. The two other pinks stay bright. But they are both significantly lighter and closer to red.

Here's a color palette I can now use to select threads and to plan my project. This palette keeps the emphasis on the multi-color and works for designs where the secondary and accent colors can be even in extent.

The second method would expend the colors found in the Byzantine ornament above. The overdye has blue, olive, gold, red, and a tiny bit of violet. All the colors are about equal in the multi-color. Any of them could be the main color. In my ornament I have already chosen blue to be the main color. If I expanded this into a larger palette I would need to decide which of the colors would be the accent (the smallest color), which would be secondary colors, and which, if any, could be ignored.

Violet is the smallest color in the multi-color but it won't make a good accent because it is too close to blue. That leaves gold, olive, and pink. Olive is also close to blue, so discard it as an accent. Both gold and pink are close to blue's complement (orange), so either could work. I would pick gold as the accent however, because it is the first color you notice in the multi-color. That makes it an excellent candidate as an accent. Olive and pink will be secondary colors and violet will be ignored.

With my ranking of colors I now have the information I need to pick threads and plan my project.

In both cases, working from the original multi-color I was able to create a cohesive color palette that tamed the original thread but still remained harmonious.

Step-by-step Instructions

This quilt is five blocks wide and six blocks high. It can be expended to be the size you like. Each block has the same structure and is stitched in **Mosaic** and **Scotch Stitches.** The central square and the four small corner squares around it are stitched in the multi-color (red lines). The corners are filled with Mosaics in the background thread (thin black lines). The block is completed with four Scotch Stitch squares in one of the coordinating thread (blue lines). A chart of the block is below.

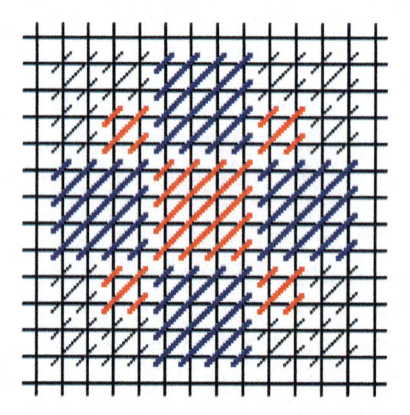

Color placement of the solid threads is important. You want most colors to be equal in extent and you do not want to create visual holes because adjacent blocks use the same color. To find the correct number of blocks per color, divide the number of colors by the number of blocks. Here that's 30/9, which is not an even number. I decided to use five blocks in my accent, four in most other colors, and to split up the remaining blocks between the other numbers.

To pick the block for a solid thread, as much as possible, I chose blocks that did not have that color in the multi-color areas. This simple precaution prevents visual holes. This gives the quilt a random look, almost as if it wasn't planned. But, in fact it is planned. The solid colors and accent were planned and taken from the multi-color. All the blocks use the same placement of colors and used the same background throughout. These two things gave a firm foundation to the project.

By using two simple rules for solid placement I was able to distribute the colors "randomly." They are: have equal or nearly equal blocks using each color, and do not have adjacent blocks that use the same solid.

As you build the quilt notice that the background corners meet up to form Greek Crosses made of Mosaic Stitches. In quilting these are called secondary patterns. In many quilts they form an exciting counterpoint to the main pattern.

Because every block is the same except for the four solid squares, the best approach for stitching this is to go row-by-row stitching the background and the multi-color for all blocks. Stitch the top background corners first. This allows you to place the multi-color stitches for that row easily. Finish up this row by stitching the bottom corner stitches in the background thread.

Once all the blocks were complete, begin to stitch the solid patches, completing one block before starting another. Based on my calculations I knew how many blocks would have patches in this color. I picked patches to fill by looking at the multi-color stitches. I used this solid color in blocks that did not have this color in the multi-color.

To pick additional patches I followed this selection process but avoided adjacent patches and tried to spread the colors out. Once I completed one color, I moved to the next.

Offset Flower

I love the look of this modern quilt design in the shape of an abstract flower. It needs a continuum of shades. Here I went from hot pink for the flower's center through yellow to shades of yellow-green. In this project, every thread is a single color; none are blended. It shows how effective solid colors can be in a design if the shading is done in a systematic way.

Another great aspect of this design is the unusual placement of the hot pink flower. By putting it outside the center, the quilt has a modern asymmetrical feel. It also gives more room for the color transition.

The original quilt used rectangular blocks paired into squares. These blocks are translated into pairs of Cashmere Stitches. In order to create squares that are always the same size, the Cashmeres should be twice as long as they are high.

Materials

1 skein each Needlepoint, Inc. silk:
    Pink:
        694 (hot pink)
        943 (pinky-peach)
    Yellow:
        868 (soft yellow-orange)
        551 (yellow)
        552 (greenish yellow)
    Green:
        651 (very pale yellow-green)
        352 (pale yellow-green)
        410 (chartreuse)
        656 (light yellow-green)
        254 (medium yellow-green)
        256 (medium-dark yellow-green)
        406 (dark yellow-green)
        298 (very dark yellow-green)
s6 inch square 18-mesh mono needlepoint canvas

PLEASE NOTE: Other threads, such as cotton embroidery floss or other brands of stranded silk, can be substituted. You can also use single strand threads for this project. Because the color sequence is the most important aspect of this quilt, a single type of thread is best for the project.

Step-by-step Instructions

The design uses a **Cashmere Stitch** that is four threads on the short side and eight threads on the long side. Any Cashmere that is twice as long as it is wide can be used. The square blocks are made from pairs of Cashmere Stitches oriented either vertically or horizontally.

The diagrams below show the two Cashmeres. Pick the stitch according to the orientation of the block.

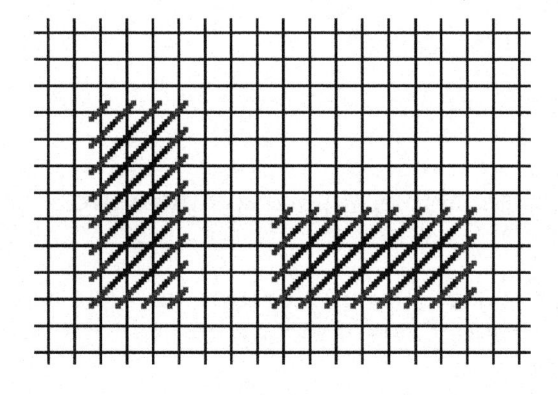

Because the stitches are all the same in the design and the color changes are subtle, I have included a layout diagram instead of a charted block. Because we know the stitch and size used for each rectangular patch, you can stitch the project from the diagram of the layout.

To make this diagram, above, easier to follow I have changed the colors to make them easier to distinguish.

Use four strands of thread throughout.

Starting about 2 ¾ " from the upper right corner, stitch the flower of four Cashmere Stitches in hot pink (694).

Following the layout diagram above, stitch a complete circle around the flower in peachy-pink (943).

Once this round is completed, blocks start to drop out. The rounds with yellow-orange (868) and yellow (551) leave out patches at the top and complete the upper right corner.

The rounds with greenish yellow (552) and very pale yellow-green (651) go ¾ around the existing stitches. After this, blocks drop out at the bottom. Pale yellow-green (352) and chartreuse (410) rounds finish out the lower right and upper left corners.

The remaining colors only go around about half the design and finish the left side and lower left corner. Stitch from light to dark: light yellow-green (656), medium yellow-green (254), medium-dark yellow green (256), dark yellow-green (406), and very dark yellow-green (298).

Triangle Tree

This ornament is based on Christmas quilts with large trees made up of triangular patches of many different kinds of green fabric. A trunk of brown is added along with white and red borders. The green threads should be mostly solid or variegated with only slight changes in color. Tweeded threads add interest while not changing color. This ornament can be stitched very quickly and makes an unusual decoration for the tree.

Materials

cream silk thread, Pepperpot would be perfect (model uses Rainbow Gallery Backgrounds "Natural Silk," - no longer made)
5 different green threads from your stash
1 skein brown matte thread (model uses Rainbow Tweed)
1 skein red variegated yarn (model uses shaded Very Velvet)
4x6 inch rectangle 18 mesh canvas

Step-by-step Instructions

Begin about 1½" from the left side of the canvas. Make the bottom row of **five-stitch triangles**, below.

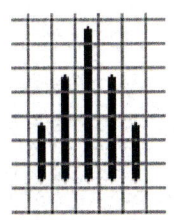

Once the bottom row is completed, continue making the tree, following the map below.

When the tree is complete, make the trunk in brown thread about seven stitches across and eight stitches long. I used **Parisian Stitch** for this, but it would also look great in Tent Stitch.

The background for the tree itself is made up of the same stitched triangles in silk. The trunk and its background is Parisian Stitch, below. There should be a half triangle (three stitches) at either side of the base of the tree.

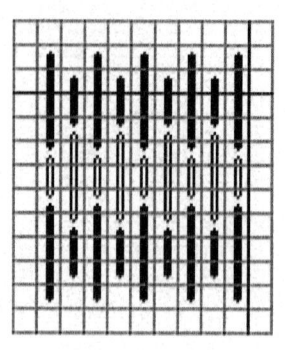

Both borders are done in **Straight Gobelin** over three threads, below. Make the red border first, and then the white border. The corners are mitered.

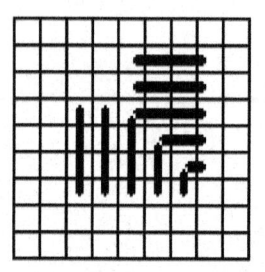

Heart Star

This project is taken from a barn quilt. These quilts are a wonderful way to decorate these utilitarian buildings. Just as barns used to have painted advertisements on them, the barn quilt movement paints on barns; but uses quilts or quilt blocks instead of ads.

Barn quilts are most popular in the Midwest, and some states even have Barn Quilt Trails for road trips to see many of them. Usually barn quilts are super-sized versions of quilt blocks, but sometimes they can be full painted quilts. Although finding more than one quilt on a barn is rare, you will see some buildings that are abundantly decorated.

Coming out of this movement is a trend in outdoor art that creates barn quilt blocks, usually about 24" square, for hanging in outdoor spaces. I am pretty sure this design is one of those pieces.

If you want to learn about barn quilts, you can read an article about them on Nuts about Needlepoint: https://nuts-about-needlepoint.com/quilt-barns-a-computer-chair-visit/

I have modified the original decoration so that it will fit into a Lee self-finishing ornament. These are 4" round and come in gold or silver or in their 4" round magnet/coaster (pictured above). It can also be finished as a 3" round ornament, finished in the Lee Needle Arts luggage tag.

Materials

1 spool Very Fine (#4) metallic in 9100 (yellow) - optional
2 spools Tapestry (#12) metallic in 9100 (yellow)
assorted threads in colors of your choice
7 inch square white 18-mesh mono canvas
Lee Needle Arts self-finishing ornament, luggage tag, or coaster

Step-by-step Instructions

The heart is made up of quartets of **Mosaic Stitches,** see full chart on page 67. There are partial quartets and single Mosaic Stitches making up the edges of the star. Use the chart, next page, to stitch the heart. All partial Mosaic Stitches are in black symbols. Full Mosaics are in a variety of colors. Please note that the stitch direction in the stitch units changes.

Once the heart is stitched and before you begin the background, with the template for your Lee round, use it to center the heart in the space and draw around it. This will define the size of your background. Use a permanent extra-fine pen made for marking fabric for this, such as a Pigma Micron.

Stitch the outer part of the ornament background in **Open T Stitch**, below, using yellow (9100) Tapestry (#12) metallic.

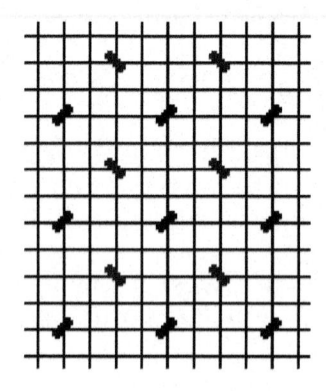

Inside the heart stitch **T Stitch,** below, using the same thread.

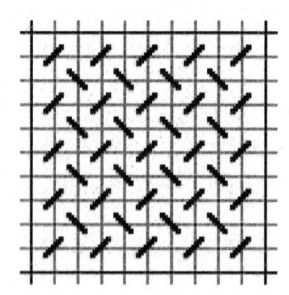

Once the center is complete, you may want to define the star's edges. Do this by outlining the outside edge of the star using the Very Fine (#4) metallic, using the Backstitch method; make one stitch for each side of the star. The model does not have this.

67

Pyramids Mini-sock

This is an example of a design taken from a one-patch quilt. All the patches are the exact same shape and size. Unlike Holiday Rickrack, another one-patch design (page 19), this project alternates background and colored triangles.

Materials

8x10 inch piece 18-mesh mono canvas
1 skein background color
1 skein accent thread in background color
20 or more scrap bag threads

Step-by-step Instructions

Using a permanent dye-base marker (like Pigma Microns or Copic markers) trace the outline of the mini-sock onto your canvas, page 70.

This pattern is based on the wonderful technique of **Trianglepoint.** Straight stitches in graduated and then decreasing lengths form an equilateral triangle. By adding more stitches you can make this pattern bigger. You can even join groups of small triangles together to make the bigger triangle used here.

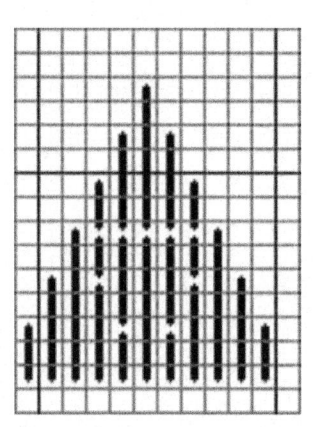

The mini-sock's triangles are made up of four five-stitch triangles, diagrammed above. A row alternates colored triangles pointing up with background triangles pointing down. With each row, the tips of the colored triangles meet the tips of the background triangles so an overall pattern is formed. You can see the structure clearly in the picture of the finished mini-sock.

Make a couple of the background triangles in the background accent thread. This enhances the scrappy look of the project.

Mini-sock Outline

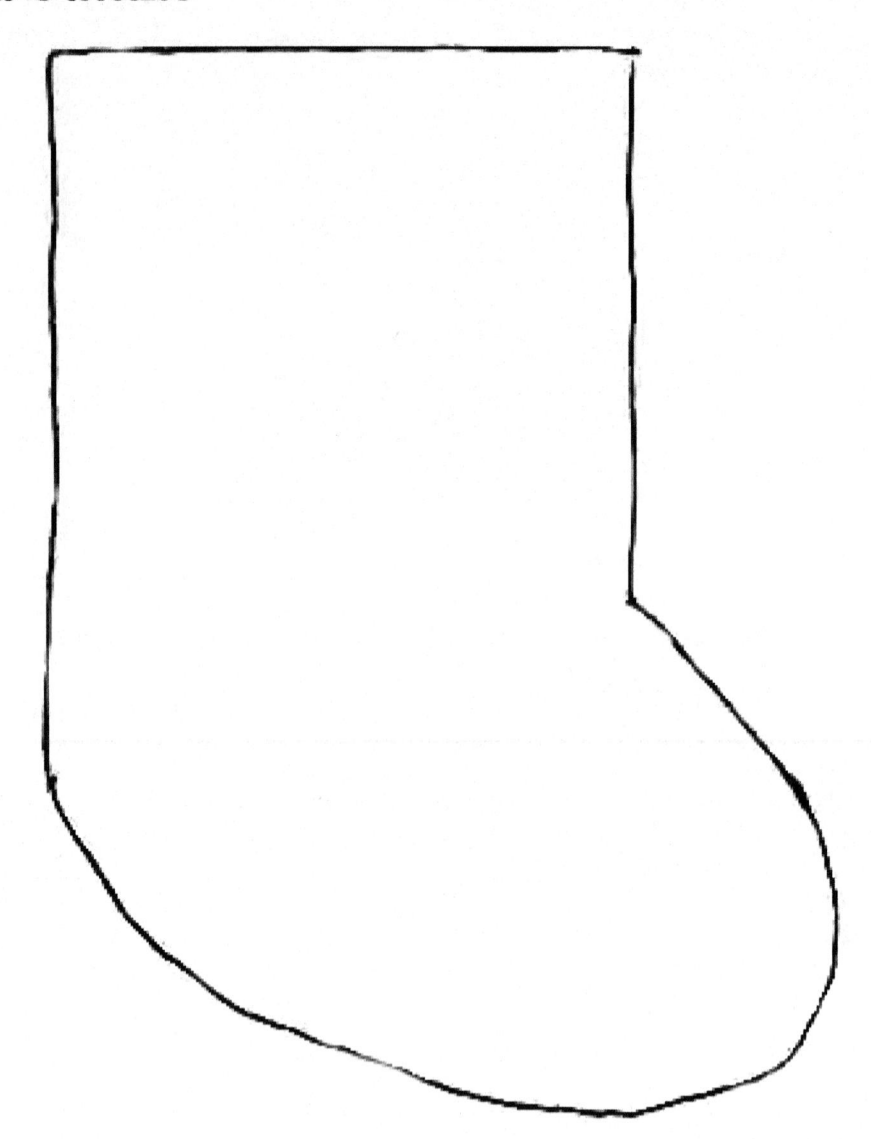

Houses

This project is taken from a scrap bag quilt that featured colorful houses. It's unusual in these projects because the background is not stitched. I intended for it to fit into this 2x3" Studio Décor frame ornament, but I counted wrong and it's too big. The instructions have you making it the size it was before I cut it. If you want to make it to fit a frame this size, leave out the sashing and the top two rows of the roofs on the upper row.

Materials

    assorted non-metallic threads from your stash
    white metallic for sashing (optional)
    6x7 inch 18-mesh bright blue canvas
    silver acrylic paint
    inexpensive bristle brush or toothbrush
    Studio Décor 2x3 ornament frame (optional)

Coloring the Canvas

The canvas I used had drips of silver paint on it. Flicking or dripping paint onto the canvas makes these. What size drips you get depends on the brush you use. If you want overall small dots use a toothbrush. If you want bigger drips, use a bristle brush, no more than ¼ inch wide.

You'll need silver metallic paint and have it thinned with water to the consistency of cream. Use a foam plate to hold the paint. This process is messy; wear old clothes and cover your work surface with several layers of newspaper. Make sure your canvas is in the middle of the paper.

Because you want drips, do not blot the paint. If you want the small dots of color, hold the paint-loaded toothbrush over the canvas. Flick your finger over the bristles of the brush, scattering the paint onto the canvas. Move the brush around and repeat the process to add more does.

For drips, hold the bristle paintbrush over the canvas and allow the paint to drip down. Once there is a drip on the canvas, use another brush to pull some of the paint away, making a blob. This process can put lots of paint of the canvas, so be prepared carefully to blot up extra paint with paper towels and to clear holes with a toothpick.

In both cases, painting is done when you like the result. Let dry overnight before stitching.

Step-by-step Instructions

All the blocks are the same and are stitched using three threads, one each for building, door, and roof. This block is a very simple house block, designed to show off threads. House blocks can, however, become quite complex. They can even be different buildings. You can even make towns and villages in quilt blocks.

The block is made up of **Scotch Stitches** over four (building and door) and various **Mosaics** and **Cashmeres** (roofs). The block diagram is pictured below. Each part of the house is represented by a different color, black for the roof, red for the building, and blue for the door,

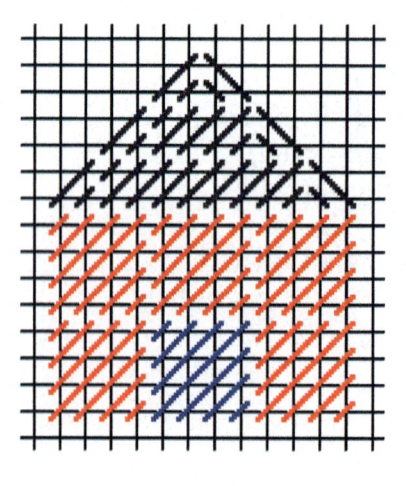

The quilt is three blocks wide and four blocks high. Between each row of blocks, you can add a row of **Tent Stitch** in white metallic as sashing. Strive to get a good distribution of colors. Do not use the same color or thread in the same place on adjacent houses.

Because the color of the canvas is intense, pick colors that are bold and bright; they will show up better. Although I did not do this, try to avoid light and medium blues for everything except the doors; they don't show up very well on this color of canvas.

This block could easily be done on a larger mesh in a bigger size to make an adorable box top, pincushion, or coaster.

Swirling Star

    This project is based on a block I found on Pinterest. It's a star block but different from the more common eight-pointed stars. Here triangles in four sizes and two colors swirl around the center diamond. This is another half-square triangle design. One stitch, Genny's Scotch, named for Genny Morrow, is used throughout. A Diagonal Gobelin border sets it off.

Materials

    2 skeins silk or cotton floss in pale shade of dominant color (background)
    1 skein overdye with areas of two distinct colors
    1 skein solid thread in one of the overdye's colors
    6 inch square 18-mesh mono canvas

Picking your Colors

The dynamic quality of this quilt block comes from the strong colors and their almost equal distribution in the overdye. When the colors are strong, it allows you to create a distinction in colors when you use one of the colors in the pair as the biggest triangles (dark grey, page 76) and the background, while the other color is the other triangles.

You force this by only using the parts of the overdye that are the chosen color (orange here) or are the transition colors (burgundy here). Only use the entire color run for the border, bringing the block together.

This overdye is an example of a color scheme I first came upon in a Japanese book on color, *Color Harmony*.. They called it Clash. Because color schemes of this kind don't always clash, I call them Near Complementary schemes.

It's easy to create these schemes. Begin with a complementary pair, such as red & green. Now move one of the pair one color away, to either red & blue or orange & green. That's a near complement. If you think about this combination you'll realize you see near complements all over. They are really popular for flags. How many flags have red and blue as the only two non-neutral colors?

If the colors in the near complement pair have equal intensity, as orange and violet have in the overdye I used, it creates a clashing scheme as long as neutral colors (i.e. white, black, and neutral grey) don't come between them. When this happens you get a vibration between the colors. Put a neutral between them, or make the intensity or value difference between them greater and the clash goes away.

You can see this by looking at two flags with near complementary schemes. The Swedish flag, below left, uses the pair of blue and yellow without a neutral. It vibrates. The Norwegian flag, below right, with the same overall structure, uses the red-blue pair. But the cross is outlined in white. The white creates a boundary and removes the clash.

Step-by-step Instructions

The block is eight stitches square. Each complete square goes over six threads. The layout of the block is shown in the map below. Black is the overdye, light grey the accent, and white the background. The blue lines indicate the breaks between stitches.

Half-Scotch triangles are not divided evenly. The longest stitch in each square is made in the dominant color. The background triangles are always the smaller half. If the overdye and the solid accent share a square, the longest stitch is done in the overdye.

Genny's Scotch, below left, and **Reverse Genny's Scotch,** below right, divide several of the longer stitches in the square. Not only does this add an internal texture to each square, it also makes the stitches less likely to snag. Use Genny's Scotch for all background triangles.

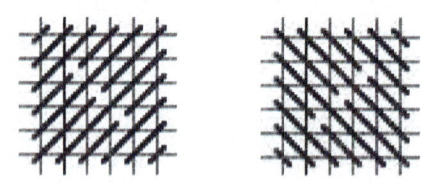

The diagrams below are in two colors to show the half-square triangle versions of both stitches.

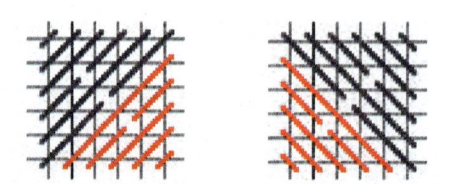

Once the background is stitched, stitch the border in **Diagonal Gobelin over 3 Threads,** below, using the overdyed thread. Use entire color runs of the thread, creating areas that alternate between the two major colors of the thread.

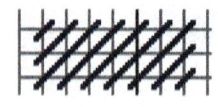

Christmas Squares

This project is a quick to stitch project that creates a charming small ornament you can finish yourself. It is in traditional Christmas colors, like a Christmas quilt, but any three-color scheme will work. I used a Studio Decor ornament frame from Michael's. They are both affordable and easy to finish.

Materials

1 card or skein cream (model uses DMC #5 Pearl Cotton in 746)
1 card or skein red (model uses Thread Gatherer Silk n'Colors in SNC 063 In the Reds)
1 card or skein green (model uses Watercolours 066 Jade)
Studio Décor 2.5" square ornament frame (available at michaels.com or in Michael's stores)
7 inch square white or sage green 18-mesh mono canvas

Step-by-step Instructions

This design repeats a simple divided square block four times to create a larger square. Sashing (a line of Tent Stitch) separates the blocks from each other.

Begin by stitching the outside of one of the blocks. These consist of two **Cashmeres** and two **Scotches** in both cream and red. These are diagrammed on the next page.

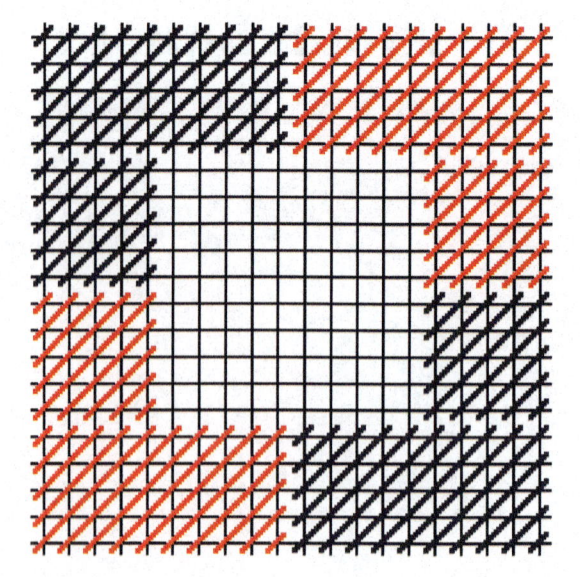

Move one thread away, for the sashing, and stitch the outside of a second block. Continue in this way until you have all four blocks stitched.

It's easiest to stitch all four centers at once in **Waffle,** below, using the green thread. Follow the numbers to create this stitch's distinctive look. Use a 24-36 inch length of thread to stitch these if possible.

Once the centers are stitched, add the sashing between the blocks in **Continental** using green. A diagram, without the centers of the entire quilt, and with the outside border, is on the next page.

79

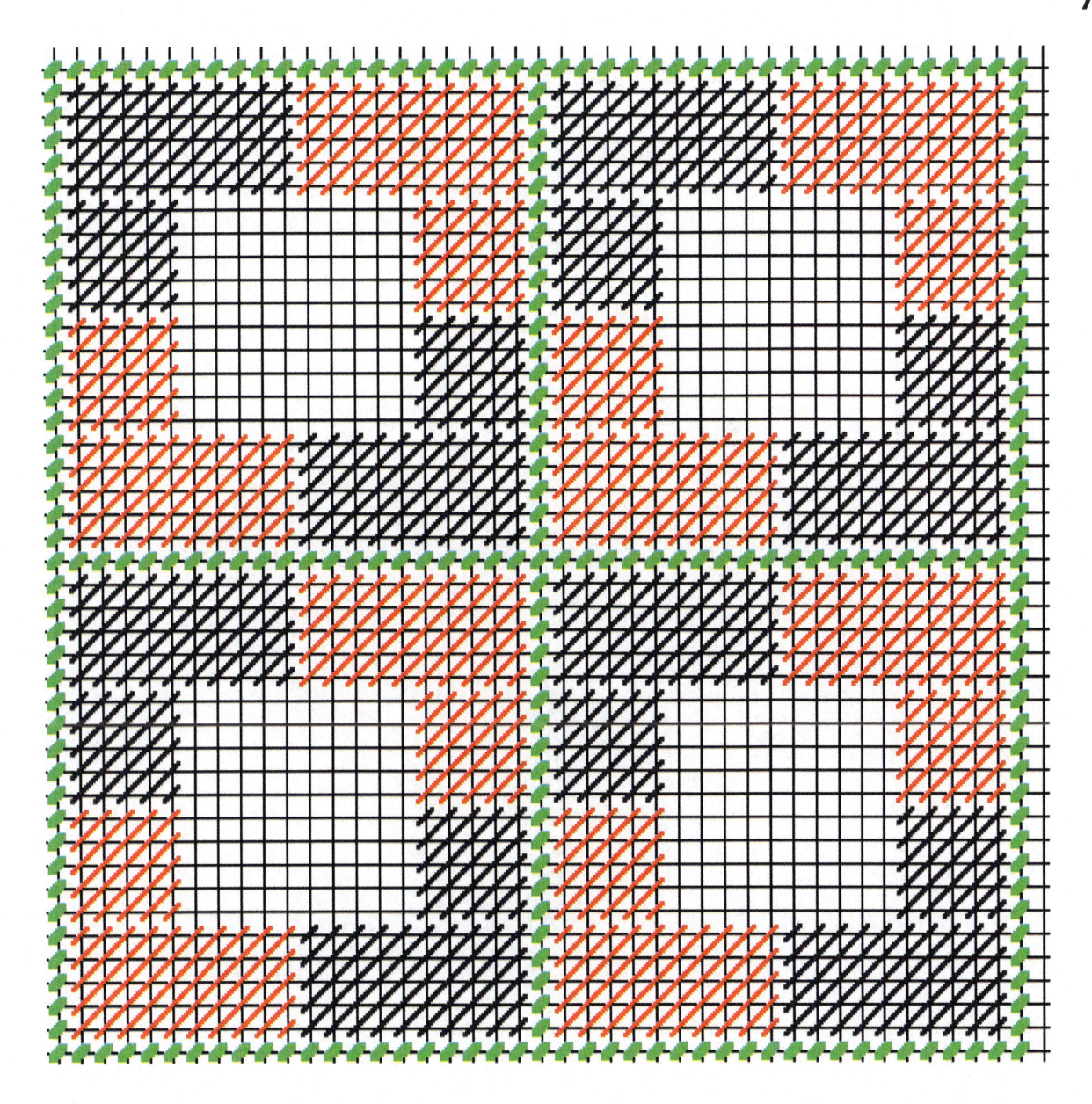

Amish Star

This project is based on a picture of an elaborate wall hanging quilt. The colorful and black half-square triangles make a series of concentric eight-point stars.

Materials

8 inch square 18-mesh mono needlepoint canvas
assorted scrap threads in background color
partial skein of black or very dark navy thread for background
Turbo Tacky Glue
black fun foam
ribbon or thread for hanger

Step-by-step Instructions

In each round, stitch the colored triangles first, and then fill in the background. I did not stop and start my scrap threads after I finished using them on a round, but parked them in the unstitched margin of the canvas.

Skip around stitching the colored triangles. This distributes the colors and threads around each round of the ornament. It does, however, make the back pretty messy.

The colored **Half Scotches** can be any color you like. I used threads in the typical Amish color palette that avoids yellow, orange, and white. To make the chart easier to follow I have done these areas in four different colors. The background stitches are all in black on the chart. These should all be black, dark grey, or navy.

While the direction of the stitches is important for the colored areas, it is not important for the background Scotches. I did not follow a consistent pattern here. Because of the dark color, the direction change is less apparent. If you were making this pattern with a light background, pick your stitch direction more carefully.

Finishing for a Quick Ornament

I love quilts that are finished as diamonds. But diamonds can be a pain to do in needlepoint. Mostly they are harder to finish. But, if you are making an ornament to hang they are much easier to hang because there are clear points for placing the hanger.

I was intrigued by a diamond ornament that attached the needlepoint to a piece of Ultrasuede or foam cut slightly larger than the needlepoint. The suede or foam created a charming border.

I completed mine using glue and fun foam. You can make yours higher quality by using Ultrasuede and sewing the needlepoint to the back.

Begin by cutting out the ornament with about a five-thread margin of unstitched canvas. Fold these edges to the back of the canvas. Run a line of glue along the stitched back of the needlepoint on one edge and press down the canvas for a minute or two until it bonds. Repeat this process with each edge. If any edges aren't sticking perfectly, weigh them down for a bit with the glue bottle. Let the whole thing rest for a couple of hours.

Take a length of ribbon about 6" or so, put the ends together and tie a knot in it to make a loop. Cut off the ends of the tie.

Place a dot of glue about ½" from a corner of the foam and put the ribbon on it.

Place glue along the edges and in a cross through the center of the needlepoint on the back. Press it onto the foam about ¼" from the corner, making sure it is even placed along the two edges of the foam.

Weigh it down and let dry for two hours. Once dry cut out the foam so that the margin of foam is even all around.

Your ornament is done.

About the Author

JANET M. PERRY is the Internet's needlepoint expert. She puts into practice her motto to make needlepoint fast, fun, and affordable.

Her exciting email classes, projects, stitch guides, and books have legions of fans worldwide. Her blogs, including Nuts about Needlepoint, are full of exciting needlepoint information. Her friendly approach helps stitchers at all levels create beautiful creative works of art. She currently runs a comprehensive needlepoint membership site, Colorful Needlepoint, which is open to new members.

This is the nineteenth book on needlepoint she has written.

Janet makes her home in the midst of lots of art and roses in a rambling house near San Francisco. She can be reached at napaneedlepoint @ gmail.com (please remove the spaces).

Printed in Great Britain
by Amazon